The Post-Conciliar Nun

The Post-Conciliar Nun

by Sister Mary Hester Valentine, SSND

CATHOLIC
PERSPECTIVES

General Editor: John J. Delaney

Hawthorn Books   *Publishers*   New York

The Post-Conciliar Nun

First Edition: 1968
Second Printing: 1968
Imprimatur

✠ Terence J. Cooke, D.D., V.G.
Archdiocese of New York
March 8, 1968

The nihil obstat and the imprimatur are official declarations that a book or pamphlet is free of doctrinal or moral error. No implication is contained therein that those who have granted the nihil obstat and imprimatur agree with the contents, opinions or statements expressed.

ACKNOWLEDGMENTS

Dylan Thomas, *Collected Poems.* Copyright 1939 by New Directions Publishing Corporation.
"Silence" from *Songs and Satires* by Edgar Lee Masters, Macmillan, 1916, 1944.
"Ash Wednesday" from *Collected Poems* by T. S. Eliot, Harcourt, Brace & World.
Hymns to the Church by Gertrud von LeFort, translated by Margaret Chanler, Sheed & Ward Inc., New York.
Excerpts from the Constitution and Decrees of the Ecumenical Council are taken from *The Documents of Vatican II,* published by Guild Press, America Press, Association Press, and Herder and Herder, and copyright 1966 by the America Press.

Contents

Introduction   7

1. The Movement Is Forward   11
2. A Splendid Heritage   26
3. Focus of Change in Religious Life   39
4. That Troublesome Vow of Obedience   47
5. "Having Nothing We Possess All Things" — The Vow of Poverty   57
6. The Cloistered Contemplative   68
7. Chastity Is Love   86
8. The Sister in Formation   96
9. After Vatican II   109

Appendices

A Decree on the Appropriate Renewal of the Religious Life (*Perfectae Caritatis*)   127
B Dogmatic Constitution on the Church (*Lumen Gentium*)—Chapter VI: Religious   146

Notes   153
Index   158

Introduction

Much has been written about the Church in the changing world; one is almost tempted to say, about the changing Church. Areas of thought and traditions which have been accepted as sacred since the Council of Trent are being challenged; re-evaluation of juridical norms has become a commonplace, and recognition of the distinction between what is of faith and what is not is a recognizable factor in the much publicized debates between theologians.

Religious life, too, in these post-conciliar years, is involved in self-examination. Following the directives in the Decree on the Appropriate Renewal of the Religious Life, religious congregations of both men and women are engaged in creative activity designed to make their witnessing to Christ more relevant to the contemporary world, their participation in the incarnation of the Church in today's culture a meaningful witness to Christ.

To write about these changes while they are in process of evolution is a difficult thing. Only a prophet can foresee where this searching re-examination will lead, and even the prophet may find that by the time his book has been written, edited, printed, and bound, with the *Imprimatur* and *Nihil Obstat* assuring its orthodoxy, his exciting news may already have slipped into the historical past and be lacking in authenticity.

Many groups are involved in the process of renovation—canon law is undergoing official scrutiny and those canons which have to do with religious life will certainly be revised. The Sacred Congregation of Religious is engaged in study of the practical aspects of renovation and in answering the questions concerning interpretation of the decree and of the *motu proprio Ecclesiae Sanctae* with which it is deluged. National Conferences of Major Superiors of both men and women are engaged in dialogue as to the best ways of meeting the challenge, and individual congregations are busy with similar discussions in general chapters and in smaller local meetings.

No generalization about 170,000 American religious women belonging to more than 400 active congregations can be taken as representative of any one of them. While each is seriously engaged in exploring possible new approaches to the original charism of the founder for the institute, not all of them are moving forward at the same rate. Discussion, even disagreement in dialogue marked the sessions of Vatican II, and out of the seemingly futile and endless debate came the sixteen official texts which have involved Catholics ever since. Any attempt to state what American sisters think or want or plan to do simply ignores the fact that, like the Bishops in Council, like any other group of people in fact, they think a great many things, have an equal variety of desires, and are still engaged in development and adjustment, processes which require an open and receptive willingness both to listen and to speak.

As in any society, there are the complacent who feel the pressures for change are the too-shrilly-articulated demands of the restless, and there are those for whom acceleration seems shod with leaden soles. And there are the others, the great majority, who listen to suggestions, weigh opinions, and who will, one suspects, be the instruments of the Spirit to adapt the best suggestions of both groups.

But in the meantime, the congregations meet, on small and local levels, in *ad hoc* committees, and in general chapters to decide what is the will of God and the Church for each of them today. The Document on Adaptation does not require uniformity in renewal; it is emphatic in stating that "communities have their own character and purpose. There-

fore loyal recognition and safe-keeping should be accorded
to the spirit of the founders, as also to all the particular goals
and wholesome traditions which constitute the heritage of
each community." [1]

This book, then, does not propose to present a blueprint
of the American convent of tomorrow. It does not represent
the decisions or thinking of the Conference of Major Superiors of Women of America, of which the author is
obviously not a member, or even of the School Sisters of
Notre Dame, of which she is. It will attempt to explore the
background of change and to point out shifting perspectives
which are now beginning to appear, if only in vague outline. The book is directed primarily to the curious layman.

.

ONE

The Movement Is Forward

The taxi driver who picked me up at the door of the college I had been visiting was silent and wary. On the way to the bus station I found him taking furtive glances at me in the mirror tilted to reflect any surprise movements of the passenger. The cab, I noted with some relief, also had a left rearview mirror in which he could observe traffic behind him.

I ventured a comment on the weather to break the all-too-obvious silence. "It is pretty warm today, isn't it?" He agreed with a monosyllable, and silence again settled in the cab, as uncomfortable as the heat on the plastic seat cover.

I tried again. "Is business better or worse in summer?"

"Just about the same except when it rains," he answered. "Then office people without umbrellas want a cab. All at the same time too." He lapsed into silence again.

Accustomed to the cheerful, garrulous Milwaukee drivers who entertain the customer with the wisdom of their eight-year-old sons, or the way they themselves put it over on good old Sister Polycarp back in the sixth grade at St. Martin of Tours, I found the present lack of communication somewhat unsettling, but made no more efforts to break the sound barrier. As he slid into the one vacant space at the depot with the competent skill of the professional, he asked the question he had obviously been carefully composing halfway across the city. "When are you going to change your clothes?"

he blurted, hiding his confusion under preoccupation with getting my bags from the car trunk into the station.

"We have changed," I answered, amused at the doubtful appraising glance he gave my ankle-length skirt, long sleeves, and veiled head. "We used to wear a great deal more starched linen veils." I demonstrated the stiff inner lining of the veil, the "cover-all" wimple.

He grinned recognition. "I know. I used to take the sisters dressed that way to the depot too. I thought you were another kind of nun. I'm not a Catholic, but I've been reading about sisters in the paper pretty much lately. They've been on TV too. They get around at lot more than they used to and I just wondered. Whether you were going on, I mean, or whether you were going into something else. Peace Corps or something like that maybe. I just wondered," he finished a bit lamely as he put my suitcase down in front of the ticket window.

"I don't know about the Peace Corps." I answered, "It may be sisters in the future will work with them, but whatever work we take up I'm reasonably sure we won't stop being nuns." He nodded (whether he understood what I meant I don't know) and left me to straighten out the tangle of a bus-train-plane trip, and to think of the thousands of individuals, Catholic and non-Catholic, who, like my taxi driver, are wondering what is going on among nuns. We are in the news certainly. A friend of mine decided to compare today's newspapers with those of a decade ago. A clipping file of stories about nuns which appeared in her local daily newspaper during one month, compared with the same paper's coverage during a month ten years ago, revealed a 51/9 ratio in favor of today — and the nine nuns who appeared in the 1956 papers were all dead, achieving only posthumous fame in the obituary columns.

Some of the reasons for the ubiquitousness of the contemporary sister, of course, have no relationship with the fact that she is a religious. Mobility is a sign of the times, the result of increased speed in transportation as well as the shift of the American population from rural to urban. Mother Theresa, the foundress who brought the first five

School Sisters of Notre Dame to the United States in 1847, was never able to cross the Atlantic again to visit her sisters and to assure herself that things were stable in this far-distant mission field. Mother Ambrosia, the congregation's present mother general, flies to the United States from Rome annually to attend the Inter-provincial Educational Conference and the Conference of Major Superiors of Women. Frequently New York is the base from which she takes off for South America or the Orient, where new mission activities demand her advice and counsel. Time has been telescoped by radio, television, cable, and phone, and the sister today lives and works in the tight little world that has emerged.

In addition to the vast technological changes of the past fifty years our era has seen rapid social changes. The UN seats newly formed states each year; countries which have been under colonial rule for centuries have achieved their independence; and our own nation is experiencing a struggle for economic and social freedom on the part of the working-man and the Negro, forcing lawmakers to confrontation with the dichotomy that exists between what the Constitution states is the basic policy of the country and what Americans actually think and do. The role of woman in twentieth century America has changed significantly from that of her mother's day, dramatically from that of her grandmother's. Today's woman has Madame Curie for a model in the area of speculative science, Clare Boothe Luce as ambassador, a comfortable number of feminine Nobel prize-winning authors to emulate, and the knowledge that 27.3 million working women make up 36 per cent of the nation's "manpower" (according to *Newsweek,* June 27, 1966). It is inevitable that young religious born and raised in this society should equip themselves for similarly wide-spread apostolates, and that they should be understandably reluctant to live and work in the circumscribed areas of an earlier era.

Viewed against the background of breath-taking social, technological, and cultural change, the shifting focus of the nun's dedicated life is not surprising. What is surprising is

the fact that the general public has been so little aware of
the slow but definite changes which have been taking place
in American convents in the past half century — that "the
emerging nun" seems to many to be exclusively post-conciliar, a phenomenon of the sixties.

Not all religious communities have met the challenge of
change to the same degree, but this is not surprising. The
civilian population also has its die-hards, and the news
coverage of Vatican II revealed to the world the varied
convictions of the bishops even in areas where a certain uniformity might have been anticipated: the study of Scripture,
the definition of the Church, the ecclesiastical powers of the
hierarchy, to mention only three. A quarter of a century ago
Rev. Daniel A. Lord, sj, made the wry comment that Roman
Catholics appeared to agree on the Apostles' Creed and then
on nothing else. It was inevitable that not all congregations
of women would agree with Pierre Teilhard de Chardin
that "In the name of our faith, we have the right and duty
to become passionate about the things of the earth," and
that these should warn their young religious about the
dangers of the world. Not all actively sense their profession
even in today's post-conciliar world as a calling from God
to a direct assignment *to the world in which they live.*

Traditions have a long life, particularly when these traditions were themselves originally a daring break with the
past. The fact that many American congregations have
European foundations explains some of the customs which
are ethnic rather than conventual in origin. Even dietary
prescriptions in the rule, when these exist, may well reflect
the country and the century of the community's origin. Our
own early enthusiasm for soup was as much a deliberate
adaptation of the food of the poor as it was the result of the
bursar's flat purse. The kissing of the episcopal ring as a
sign of loyalty to the bishop, only recently dropped by some
American bishops, had its counterpart in many convents in
the kissing of a superior's hand when receiving assignments.
It was a custom which, while peculiarly distasteful to
Americans, roused no resentment in countries where the
kissing of the hand was an ordinary sign of respect. I recall

my acute embarrassment as a young nun when the Hunga-
rian mother of a student bent over the hand I had stretched
to her in greeting and gave it the customary courteous kiss.

Traditions in religious communities are not all European
born, of course. One American-founded congregation had
until recently three deep tucks in the skirt of the habit,
which in the early days were unstitched at the time of the
wearer's death, providing sufficient cloth to cover the corpse's
feet in an open coffin. Shoes obviously were too expensive to
be taken to the grave when there were other living feet they
would fit.

Some of the customs which have been receiving considerable publicity in *The National Catholic Reporter,* as well
as in other periodicals that give space to the contemporary
sister and her problems, are based upon the code of canon
law for religious, not on the rule or constitutions of the
sisters. An example of such is the practice of having a
companion sister when traveling outside the cloister which
has only recently been mitigated for America. Although
many critics have pointed out that the American sister does
not need either the protection or the chaperonage of the
companion, what they fail to recognize is that the regulation
may well have served as a safeguard in a more hostile
environment.

But there is no blinking at the fact that some customs
officially approved when the rules and constitutions of
religious women were examined by the Sacred Congregation
of Religious in 1924 were obsolete even then. Electricity is
so much a part of life in the United States that even at the
beginning of this century to warn the sisters of the dangers
of lamps and candles would appear to be unnecessary. One
canon lawyer, when asked how such clearly inappropriate
regulations passed the eagle eye of the board of canonists
appointed to the reading of the rules, pointed out that even
today there are areas where electricity is not a commonplace, where sisters, especially those whose communities
have establishments in these underprivileged parts of the
world, might well be warned of the risks of fire. He also
admitted, a bit ruefully, that since canonists are human,

they may well have missed some points all too obvious later. Hindsight always has 20/20 vision.

It is to deal with these anachronisms as well as to reassess the aims of the communities in the light of today's needs that Rome asked them to examine their rules and constitutions in general chapter by 1968, making such changes as the needs of the contemporary apostolate seem to demand. And, in response to an almost universal restlessness with outmoded customs, changes there will certainly be. A look at the past will show that sisters have long engaged in activities that are being now proposed as peculiarly modern. Emergencies may have called them into being, but the fact remains that sisters did leave their much more rigidly cloistered convents during the cholera and influenza epidemics to nurse the sick in their homes. Floods, fires, and wars have found the sisters actively engaged in relieving the misery of the homeless and afflicted. The chronicles of every religious institute tell of the sharing of meager provisions with the poor. San Francisco has never forgotten the work of nuns during its great earthquake of 1906, as New Orleans has not forgotten their dedication to the victims of yellow fever.

The updating of religious may well widen the area of this service. The insights contemporary theology, psychology, and sociology have given us may permit the modern nun to see the world with keener vision, to sense its reality more clearly, and to evaluate her own responsibility with more distinct consciousness; but she will always find counterparts in the past of her congregation; her own potentialities will develop best on the solid foundation of a tradition of service already history.

The present restless period may well be a time of crisis, but rather than cause panic it ought to engender optimism. Denouement logically follows crisis — and pain is a sharp reminder that the body is alive.

Even though Pope John XXIII's open-window policy was not an entirely new concept (the awareness of the need for greater involvement in the problems of the contemporary world has been apparent in greater or less degree in the encyclicals of the Popes of the past century), there is no question about the acceleration engendered by his plea for *aggiornamento* and his convoking of the Council. The last decade has been marked with a decisive increase in personalism in all areas: in liturgy, in Scripture study, in collegiality of the bishops and the involvement of the people of God, the laity, in the work of the Church. The Catholic of the sixties, and the nun no less than her lay sister, has a new realization of her individual commitment, what Karl Rahner calls "the freedom of acceptance or refusal of salvation which occurs in all the dimensions of human existence, and occurs always in an encounter with the world, not merely in the confined sector of the sacred or of worship and 'religion' in the narrow sense. It occurs in encounters with one's neighbor, with one's historical task, with the so-called world of everyday life, in and with what we call the history of the individual and of communities." [1] She realizes that she has a duty toward history, that she must make and suffer history, and in that realization is confirmation of her conviction that an exclusively private interest in her own salvation is no longer possible, if it ever was.

Nothing that concerns others is unrelated to her apostolate, as the *Decree on the Appropriate Renewal of the Religious Life* points out. Not even the most conservative of religious will argue the isolationist thesis, but adaptation to a world whose technological changes are so rapid that the plane which makes its test flight today is already outdated by the blueprints of its successor presents problems that call for daring and prudence, fortitude and wisdom of almost superhuman proportions. There are those who ask whether religious life is even relevant to our times, whether a new form of oblation to God through service will not emerge during the next century. There are those who wonder whether the structure of religious life as we know it is flexible enough to contain within itself the expanding needs of the future, whether the multiple areas in which the sister apostle of the future will work can be contained within the framework of rules drawn up for the comparatively structured patterns of teaching, nursing, and the social service of the past.

It is not easy to differentiate between superficial criticism for the sake of criticism and legitimate questions regarding renewal, with their concommitant serious concern for interpretation of the mind of the Church.

When one considers the various reactions of "good Catholics" to the post-conciliar liturgical changes: the nostalgic, puzzled, and sometimes violent "letters to the editor," the delay in adaptation on the part of many pastors and even an occasional bishop, the formation of Father De Pauw's bitter traditionalist group, it is not surprising that talk of possible changes in their way of life should find some religious women hesitant and not a little worried about the future. Nor are these individuals always the secure, the timorous, the middle-aged. Many are those who last year, or in the last decade, made the great renunciation to God, and who are spending themselves in steady, quiet, daily oblation in a well-known pattern, tried and defined over centuries. There is no clear line by which those with confidence, verve, poise, laughter, zest for life, and love of Christ can be classified. Many sisters who have been the salt of their communities, who have measured up bravely in the past, are confused by the unknown in these times of swift change, when the way of life they know may break off and a new, untried way may begin. It is not that they are satisfied with the old, but that they do not see where the proposed new is leading them. Father Leen pointed out in *In the Likeness of Christ* that few if any religious reach middle age in a spirit of complacency. But there is assurance that the past with all its weaknesses produced heroic women, saints — will the new proposed ways of life have the same potential?

The nun of today is living in a pioneer age that challenges all the frontiers of the human spirit. The majority of sisters are perfectly willing to cross those frontiers when the objectives are made clear. As one of my colleagues said, "I'm willing to go any place I am sent, to do any job to which I am assigned and for which I am prepared — but I hope we know where we are going before we start."

It is a valid desire, and one which the Conferences of Major Superiors of Women, both here and in Europe, are attempting to satisfy, as is the Sacred Congregation of Religious which has already drawn up the blueprint for the "new life" in the *Decree on the Appropriate Renewal of the Religious Life* and in Chapter VI of *De Ecclesia*. That the ground plan will need explanation is clear, that as the Constitution on the Liturgy left the adaptation of its principles to the local bishops in order that the peculiar needs of the culture of the country might be met, so too, whatever guidelines are presented for the sisters' consideration, flexibility will be of primary importance. Since sisters, too, work in many lands and in varied cultural and economic situations, any rule which does not recognize the quite differing needs arising out of these circumstances will be impractical and may, in fact, frustrate the very ends for which it was formed. For example, one has only to consider the limited social opportunities of women in many areas [the visit of Faisal of Saudi Arabia during which wives of American state officials were not welcome at formal dinners given in his honor in Washington [2] has underscored the subservient place of woman in at least one area of the world] to realize the unfavorable impression freedom of movement might have on the native population.

Orientals respect age, and our congregation has discovered that on Guam the older stateside superior is more acceptable than a younger woman, even though the latter might be more knowledgeable in the language and customs of the island.

Someone has remarked that the pioneers always surveyed the land before building the railroad. Whatever changes the various congregations of religious women finally adopt will be effective because the land, "white with the harvest" and waiting for the reapers, has been carefully studied and its needs assessed.

Part of the problem for many American communities lies in the fact that they have anticipated the decree. The Sister Formation movement, about which we shall speak later, was itself a farsighted and clearheaded approach to the training of active religious for their professional work. Additional change comes hardest to those who have just completed a program of self-evaluation which culminated in radical and important revisions of both program and purpose.

The last half dozen years have witnessed a vital surge for self-identity within the convent as well as outside. There is a healthy dialogue concerning the contemporary interpretation of the vows; the witness of poverty; the significance of the habit; the value of co-operative action with lay bodies.[3] There is a healthy airing and occasionally a decided clash of opinion. For every Mary Perkins Ryan who questions the effectiveness of the Catholic school system there is a Greeley report justifying it by pointing to its strengths as well as its weaknesses. The Catholic hospital is undergoing scrutiny. Would it be better for the sisters to turn the administration (and the ownership) of the hospitals over to a lay board and fulfill the apostolate of mercy more immediately as bedside nurses? Will Medicare so increase the sister supervisor's work that human contact with the suffering is drastically curtailed?

Does the work of the sister in Newman centers and on state university campuses, where several are already witnessing to Christ by their scholarship, foreshadow the wider educational apostolate of the future which a pluralistic society demands? In what does the social mission of religious in South America consist?

There are few communities in which the tension between participation in society and withdrawal from it is not making itself felt. The recognition of our need to act in the world as a complementary force, to work with men of good will, is not, however, a fresh point of view. The false concept that there is a polarity between commitment to God and to man was destroyed forever by Christ, who identified the two great Commandments of the Law: "Thou shalt love the Lord thy God with thy whole heart, with thy whole soul, with thy whole strength and with thy whole mind, *and* thou shalt love thy neighbor as thyself." How this is to be accomplished is the task of each generation to work out in terms of its own situation.

At a conference of the National Union of Italian Superiors, May 1966, Pope Paul VI spoke of the principles upon which effective adaptation of the religious life must be based. "And do you love the Church? the Church of the Council which desired to examine all the problems of modern life with openness for the salvation of souls? In what spirit have you accepted the invitation for renewal, and with what trust have you accepted the directives of the Church?" The Pope gave three specific directives as a procedural formula:

1. conscious participation in the Sacred Liturgy, particularly in the mystery of the Eucharist in accordance with the mind of the Church;

2. familiarity with the books of the Old and New Testament, so that nourished by these they might love the other members of Christ's body as brothers;

3. Community spirit which will not be lacking when the foundation posts of Liturgy and Scripture are solidified.[4]

This is, of course, an adaptation of his message to the Council fathers in the final session, "From now on, *aggiornamento* will signify for us a wisely undertaken quest for a deeper understanding of the spirit of the Council, and the faithful application of the norms it has happily and prayerfully provided."[5] The charters for renewal and change in religious life lie in the sixteen official texts promulgated by the Ecumenical Council. For this reason religious communities are engaged in serious dialogue and study not only on the Chapter VI of *De Ecclesia* and the *Decree on the Appropriate Renewal of the Religious Life,* both of which specifically deal with their way of life, but with all sixteen of the official texts which point out the total mission of the Church to witness, ministry, and fellowship.

Renewal of the individual, of religious congregations, and of the entire Church, is undertaken only that each may be found faithful to the gospel of Christ. Religious, belonging as they do to the people of God, are not separate from but distinctly a part of the total community as the position of the section dealing with them in the *Dogmatic Constitution on the Church* clearly indicates. Someone has pointed out that the Levites in the Old Testament were chosen, not for any special qualifications they themselves might possess, but that they might serve as a constant reminder to the Chosen

People of God's relationship to the nation. As he sometimes raised up to himself prophets to be his mouthpiece, so God had chosen the Levites for his special service and so might he, were it his will, require of all those whom he has made, a similar complete dedication. That this selection was to serve as a sign, and that this separation was not to make the one so chosen insensitive to duties, anxieties, and suffering is clearly stated in Leviticus, and repeated with divine insistence in the parable of the good Samaritan. The comparative isolation into which religious life moved is partly the result of historical forces which will be explained later.

The description of the priestly people which occurs in *De Ecclesia* in the section on the laity: "The faithful join in the offering of the Eucharist by virtue of their royal priesthood. They likewise exercise that priesthood by receiving the sacraments, by prayer and thanksgiving, by the witness of a holy life, and by self-denial and active charity," [6] is also a description of the scaffold upon which all religious congregations are based. The Rule and Constitutions of the Congregation of the School Sisters of Notre Dame, for example, has chapters on Community Prayer, Love for the Most Blessed Sacrament, Meditation, Practices of Penance, and Charity. That the specific means by which these identical and universal objectives are to be attained differs not only between the laity and religious, but also between congregation and congregation, is not surprising, but the inevitable result of the individual charismatic gift by which "all the faithful, whatever their condition or state are called by the Lord, each in his own way, to that perfect holiness whereby the Father himself is perfect." The sister's way of life is one "tending toward holiness by a narrower path," but always so that she may "stimulate by . . . example." [8]

The sister today is planning seriously for the work of tomorrow. There is no doubt that her apostolate will involve more social areas than in the past; in fact, even though she is professionally a teacher or a nurse, she has already taken on service which a decade ago would have been reserved for the social worker. The emphasis of Vatican II on the missionary Church and its involvement in the non-Christian community is bound to have far-reaching effects upon the apostolate of the active religious. It is essential that the shift of emphasis or change of purpose, where this is the considered decision of the congregation, be based upon a thorough understanding of current needs, an intellectual grasp of the complications involved in contemporary urban problems. Whether one agrees with all the proposals Harvey Cox makes in *The Secular City,* there can be no quarrel with his analysis of our national shift from a rural to an urban society. The emerging social and political problems of this new complex world demand new solutions in keeping with this new social reality.

Any simplistic approach which attempts to use the remedies of the past for the social ills of today is bound to be disastrous. Even government, with its facilities for research and study, its available funds for implementing plans proposed by experts, has found itself unable to cope adequately with the complexities of urban renewal, adequate education for all America's children, rising unemployment, and civil rights.

In addition to a warm Christ-like affection for the underprivileged, the sister must have an intellectual grasp of the economic and social factors which have built the walls behind which the large majority of the world's population lives. Cox is not the only student of the current scene to wonder whether the Church-sponsored youth groups that generously give themselves to cleaning, painting, and making more livable the wretched rooms of tenement dwellers are not unconsciously serving to perpetuate the situation instead of alleviating it. Landlords who should take responsibility for decent housing are relieved of their obligation, and the poor who have neither money for the repairs that the group provided nor the physical energy needed to achieve them are made to feel that, somehow, the failure is theirs. Cox suggests that a more effective and permanent program might have been achieved if the young people had made a group study of the factors which perpetuate slum conditions, and in the strength of their knowledge had approached local and legislative power in the community, respectfully agitating for specific action to be taken.

Although there will always be need for person-to-person contact, there is the real danger that isolated assistance to individuals may serve as a Band-Aid for society's cancer. As Cox has pointed out, the Church can do certain things, but it cannot do some of the things which must be accomplished by industrial missions and issue-oriented groups. "The real question is how this fund of resources can be channeled into a ministry of exorcism in the city." [9] The sister serving the disadvantaged today must become involved in all the agencies through which social reform can be implemented.

There are areas opening before the American nun whose apostolic potential has scarcely been tapped. This does not necessarily mean that all communities should engage in all of these; in fact, multilateral activity may so dissipate the energies of a congregation as to endanger not only its works and focus, but its existence. In an age of specialization, congregations will not try to do everything that is to be done. The major works of each will grow from self-study which evaluates the talents, background, and training of existent personnel, its established institutions and professional reputation, and the apostolic works of the Church as well as the discerned needs in those areas to which it has access.

There will be crises of choice, inevitably, and expanding of commitments. But expansion does not mean dropping the established works of education, the care of the sick, the old, the mentally retarded.

One of the objectives of a community self-study is the realistic appraisal of the weaknesses of the system and the resultant failure to achieve already established goals. An increased social awareness with specific teaching of the moral obligation of individuals to exercise justice in actual current situations will follow, one hopes, the revelation of the inadequacies of our past teaching in this area which the 1966 civil rights riots in Chicago and other cities demonstrated. Both the teacher and the nurse will reassess their personal contacts with the people of God. Both work with the neglected, with those whose lives are empty of love. The opportunity to make important individual Christian contacts in these cases has too frequently been bypassed in the interests of "professional" duties. The child is more important than the lesson, and the patient more important than the record—although there is no reason why planning linked to dedication should not manage both. It may require a reapportionment of duties; there are those who prophesy that the Catholic school of the future as well as the hospital will be administered by the laity. Perhaps that is the solution, but only serious study of the multifaceted problem will provide even tentative answers.

Change there will be, perhaps radical, perhaps less so, but it is good for us to remember Thomas More's wise comment in a similar transitional era: "There is not an old church of Christ and his apostles, and another new Church now, but one whole Church from that time to this time in one truth continued." [10]

TWO

A Splendid Heritage

What do we mean by religious? Almost any adult Catholic to whom the question is put feels qualified to give an answer, since all have a vague and general idea that it is a life directed to personal perfection, or a life seeking union with God. Yet in all ages and places these two aspects exist in more or less intensity in all religions. Roman history introduces the student to the vestal virgin in whose cloister layout Van Zeller sees the architectural prototype of the Christian nunnery.[1] The news photographer covering the bitter Vietnamese war has familiarized Americans with the saffron-robed Buddhist nun with her begging bowl.

The fact that outside the Church, women dedicate their lives to a life of renunciation and prayer should be no cause for wonder.[2] Neither should we conclude, however, that Christian monasticism is derived from their example; resemblance cannot be equated with identity, as Newman pointed out in his comments on the similarity between Christian truth and its rudiments or its separate parts, as found in heathen philosophies and religions. "We say, and we think that Scripture bears us out in saying, that from the beginning, the Moral Governor of the world has scattered the seeds of truth far and wide over its extent: that these have variously taken root, and grown up as in the wilderness, wild plants indeed but living." [3] While there are similarities between the non-Christian ˙nun and the Catholic

sister, the difference is all the difference. The special consecration of the Christian nun is founded on revelation. This
consecration of religious vowing observance of the evangelical counsels is a bond by which individuals are "totally
dedicated . . . and committed to the honor and service of
God under a new and special title" (#44).

While religious life as it has developed in the church was
unknown in the Old Testament, there seem to have been
religious women who voluntarily attached themselves to the
temple service. The aged Anna, who with Simeon welcomed
Christ at his presentation in the temple, is referred to with
respect, with a casualness which would seem to indicate that
she was not the first to dedicate her widowhood to abiding
"continually in the temple night and day, serving God with
fasting and prayer" (Lk 2:36). St. Luke, listing the followers of Our Lord, mentions certain women "who ministered
to him with the means they had" (Lk 8:3), and St. John
gives the account of the first apostle to the apostles, Mary
Magdalen, who "brought news to the disciples of how she
had seen the Lord and he had spoken to her" (Jn 20:18).
None of these women fits into the pattern of contemporary
religious life (even though Gallic legend has Mary Magdalen
the first French nun in her cell near Marseilles!), but it is
the tradition of their personal service to Christ which is the
source from which all active religious derive. St. Paul makes
frequent mention of women in the early Church who gave
abundantly of themselves (Lydia, Acts 16:14–15; 40) or who
made long journeys (Phoebe, Rom 16:1–2) or who taught
and instructed (Prisca and Aquila, Rom 16:3–4). And St.
Peter raised Dorcas, the head of a little circle of Christian
seamstresses, from the dead (Acts 9:36–43). It was not, however, to these any more than to the legendary companion of
St. Paul, Thecla, who, according to the apocryphal Acts of
St. Paul founded the first convent at Seleucia in Asia Minor,[4]
that the Council refers when it reminds us that "from the
very infancy of the Church there have existed men and
women who strove to follow Christ more freely and imitate
him more nearly by the practice of the evangelical counsels"

(Decree on the Appropriate Renewal of the Religious Life, #1).

Strictly speaking, even the convent at Bethlehem established in the fourth century by that astonishing friend of St. Jerome, St. Paula, was not one. Although it has been called the Mother of Convents, Paula and her saintly companions took no formal vows. Their lives of prayer, penance, study, and service in the hospital and school superintended by St. Jerome have a good many parallels with the form of conventual life drawn up by St. Benedict a century later, and the letters of St. Jerome reveal quite a twentieth century awareness of feminine competence. His request that Paula, "so familiar with Hebrew literature and so skilled in judging the merits of a translation, go over this one carefully, word by word, so as to discover where I have added or omitted anything which is not in the original," [5] comes close to duplicating the recent approbation Rev. Andrew Greeley gave to nun specialists in his own field of sociology. "At the 1966 meeting of the American Catholic Sociological Society," said Father Greeley, "in theoretical approach, in methodological sophistication and social commitment (in fashion once again among sociologists), the sister sociologists were always excellent and on occasion brilliant." [6]

The location of the first convent, as well as the name of its founder, is lost in the mist of history. We know that St. Scholastica's sixth century convent, based upon her brother Benedict's modification of the Eastern system of monasticism which had arisen in the Egyptian deserts in the third century, was not the first convent in the Western church. In Ireland there were "nunneries" founded by St. Bridget in the fifth century, and St. Martin of Tours is also credited with having founded congregations of religious women under vows. While these early convents undoubtedly served as refuge for the women of those turbulent times, it is equally clear from the records that they recognized that the grace of Catholicism and vocation were not given to them for themselves alone, but were bestowed for the benefit of their brethren in the world.

According to Henry Adams, medieval woman was the

determining force in the civilization of the Middle Ages. Certainly the spirited nuns and clear-sighted abbesses had an appreciation of the possibilities opening out to them, and turned these to account in surprisingly versatile fashion. St. Hilda of Whitby, whom the Venerable Bede immortalized in his account [7] of her handling of the first English poet, Caedmon, was not only the head of the double monastery of monks and nuns, but was an official member of the important Council of Whitby in 664. The modern nun wonders whether any monastery of men today would elect the superior of the neighboring convent as the person best qualified to handle the affairs of the monastery, as was Aethelburg, abbess at Barking. That these men were not weak-minded individuals content to rest under the maternal care of a strong abbess is evident from the fact that five of the men of St. Hilda's monastery were promoted to the episcopate. Foremost among them was John, Bishop of Hexham (687–706) and afterwards of York (721), and the famous St. John of Beverley of whose activities Bede has left an account.

Nuns were conspicuously absent in the opening sessions of Vatican II, but at the Council of Beaconsfield in 694, five abbesses were present, all of them with the right of vote. In a charter of privileges granted between 696 and 716 by King Wihtred and Queen Werburg to the churches and monasteries of Kent, granting them security against interference, five lady abbesses placed their signatures to the document. Judging from the place given to them, they ranked in dignity below the bishops but above the presbyters whose names follow theirs in the list. In Germany abbesses ranked among the independent princes of the Empire and voted in the Diet as members of the Rhenish bench of bishops, either in person or by proxy.

The early missionaries like the missionaries of the twentieth century were reluctant to establish centers without the co-operative help of the nuns. St. Boniface's missionary endeavors for Germany were strengthened by the presence of St. Lioba and her nuns, who left England to found the convent at Bischofsheim. Both St. Amand in Holland and

St. Winebald in Germany depended upon their co-adjutors, Sts. Adeltrudis and Walburgis, in their Christianizing of the tribes, particularly in the education of women.

When Vatican II recommended that religious "take the sacred Scriptures in hand each day by way of attaining the excelling knowledge of Jesus Christ through reading these divine writings and meditating on them," [8] it was simply emphasizing a tradition that has been a part of conventual life from the beginning. An early biographer of St. Lioba reports that "she zealously read the books of the Old and New Testaments, and committed their divine precepts to memory; but she further added to the rich store of her knowledge by reading the writings of the Holy Fathers, the canonical decrees, and the laws of the Church." [9] St. Gertrude of Helfta of Eisleben, Saxony, wanted girls instructed in the liberal arts, for she felt that if knowledge were to perish they would no longer be able to understand holy writ, and religion together with devotion would disappear. When one realizes that at this time few men other than clerics could do more than sign their names, the literacy of these cloistered women is particularly remarkable.

It was inevitable that these convent schools should produce authors who would themselves write the books whose lack they had deplored. Ealdhim wrote a treatise for Barking in the eighth century which indicated a high degree of culture attained by the women for whom it was destined. In it he praises the nuns as gymnosophists and scholars. Hroswitha, "the strong voice of Gandersheim," is famous for her metrical legends, her metrical versions of contemporary history, and the seven metrical dramas which are the only dramatic compositions we have between the comedies of classic times and the miracle plays. A less well-known but perhaps more representative example of the conventual playwright producing edifying dramas for feast days is St. Hildegard of Bingen, who wrote allegorical dramas on the progress of the soul on the way to heaven. Interestingly enough she also wrote two books on medicine, one of which went into several editions as late as the sixteenth century.

Herrad, the abbess of Hohenburg in the twelfth century, conceived the idea of compiling for the use of her nuns an encyclopedic work which would embody in pictures and in words the knowledge of her age. The importance of this work has long survived the attainment of its original purpose, for with its hundreds of illustrations and its copious text it has afforded a wealth of information on the customs, manners, conceptions, and mode of life of the twelfth century to which many students of archaeologoy, art, and philology have gone for instruction and for the illustration of their own books.[10]

The invention of the printing press provided the means for multiplication of books, and in Florence one of the earliest and finest printing presses was established in 1476 in the convent of the Dominican nuns, with St. Jacob di Rivoli and the sisters as the first compositors, turning out serious and important publications.

There is a decidedly modern awareness of contemporary apostolic needs in the chronicles of religious houses of women in the Middle Ages, and history has a way of debunking the generally accepted theory that theirs was a life out of contact even with the isolated world of their day. *The National Catholic Reporter* (September 14, 1966) carried a story of a two-day conference in London of some sixty women from seven countries who were making new efforts to get permission for women to become priests. They particularly urged that Canon 968, which states that only a baptized man is eligible for the priesthood, should be changed to read a *baptized person*. The only twentieth-century aspect of this convention is the fact that they were addressed by Archbishop Igino Cardinale, apostolic delegate to Britain, who told them not to let up in their agitation for equal rights in the Church. "I think it is right," he said, "for you to put to the Holy See any idea you feel to be reasonable and to have it evaluated. As regards canon law, I think it is a very good thing to make the representations you have already made."

A similar gathering in the early thirteenth century was castigated by Brother Berthold, an influential preacher of south Germany, who spoke ardently against women who would officiate at divine service and gave a detailed analysis of the mischief that might result from such a course.[11]

The current debate on religious garb has a similarly ancient and honorable history. There is extant a highly interesting pamphlet written about the year 1190 by a monk, Idung, in Bavaria, which shows that professed religious women in the district did not wear a distinctive dress. He ends his pamphlet with the amusing advice that as it is impossible to interfere with the liberty of nuns, it should at least be obligatory for them when away from home to wear clothes which would make their vocation obvious.[12]

All of these early convents were more or less autonomous, following with local adaptations the flexible rule of St. Benedict or the more rigid ones of the Gaelic founders if they were not loosely affiliated under the rule of St. Augustine. In the thirteenth century a new form of religious life for women came into existence in the mendicant order of Poor Clares. As the earlier communities were born in answer to a particular need of their time, the new congregation of St. Francis and St. Clare also served to witness a special aspect of the Gospel which had become buried under the corporate possessions of endowed monasteries both of men and of women.

Although the mendicant friars spread their message of detachment and poverty on the highways and in the cities, their second orders—St. Dominic's foundation for women at Prouille and St. Francis' under the direction of St. Clare at Assisi—remained strictly cloistered.

There were, of course, practical as well as spiritual reasons for this. Pope Boniface VIII in his famous constitution *Periculoso* not only forbade religious women to leave the enclosure lest the purpose for which they entered the monastic life be endangered, but restricted the entrance of the laity into the cloister. To the contemporary mind there is something of an anomaly in the idea that the works of Christ might separate from him, but the Carmel in which the young St. Teresa of Avila was professed is ample testimony of the decline of dedication in monasteries where enclosure had been relaxed. One suspects, too, that Chaucer's Dame Eglantyne was not the only prioress to go on pilgrimage with some decidedly dubious companions. At any rate the post-Reformation decrees of the Council of Trent in 1645 ordered that "the enclosure of nuns be restored wherever it has been violated, and that it be preserved where it has not been violated." [13] The Council adds, "And since monasteries of nuns situated outside the walls of a city and town are often without any protection, exposed to the rapacity and other crimes of evil men, the bishops and other superiors shall make it their duty to remove, if they deem it expedient, the nuns from those places to new or old monasteries within cities or more populous towns. . . ." [14]

It was this regulation which forced St. Francis de Sales and St. Jane Francis de Chantal to give up their plans for the Visitation's nursing apostolate, shifted the Ursuline educational emphasis, and suppressed the institute which Mary Ward had so patiently built up. St. Peter Fourier, who in 1597 received the first School Sisters of Notre Dame, found his plans for small convents in which a few sisters might take over the Christian education of poor children in villages and hamlets conflicting with the prescription that monasteries should be built within cities or more populous towns. Small towns and villages could not support a large monastery, and without the sisters the children of the middle and lower classes remained largely uninstructed. It was an impasse which many generous, apostolic souls faced as the needs of the poor of Christ cried out for their attention, an impasse which St. Vincent de Paul solved for Louise de Marillac and the Daughters of Charity by insisting that they were not religious. "Religious must needs have a cloister, but the Sisters of Charity must go everywhere." As Bishop Huyghe has pointed out,[15] the entire history of the orders and congregations is one long struggle between the stability and rigor of the law and the thrusts of life which, in the face of the immense and varied tasks confronting the Church, requires them to receive religious consecration without submitting to juridical conditions unsuited to them.

In order to meet the needs of the post-Reformation

Church a vast number of associations, societies, third orders, and congregations came into existence which, because their members took simple, not solemn, vows if they took vows at all, did not come under the canonical classification of religious and hence were able to work under a more mitigated rule of enclosure than the older traditional orders. Official recognition of this type of religious life was achieved in the middle of the eighteenth century when Pope Benedict XIV allowed to the institute of the English Virgins most of the privileges which had been denied the seventeenth century founders, and in so doing unofficially approved all similar congregations. Leo XIII gave these canonical status by his constitution, *Conditae a Christo.*[16] The immediate result was a burst of local foundations born of specific needs and the reluctance of local ordinaries to sponsor congregations with headquarters and government in a distant diocese over which they would have no control.

Although a group of French Ursulines landed in New Orleans in 1727 to found the first Catholic school for girls in America, only five of the communities of women now working in the United States had convents here earlier than the beginning of the nineteenth century. This is understandable, since Roman Catholics were a tolerated minority in the original colonies with the exception of Maryland, and adventurers who were attracted to the vast wilderness of the West were not likely to invite sisters to accompany them on their pioneering ventures.

Two factors appear to have been influential in attracting religious congregations of women to the United States: anticlerical laws in their native lands, and the changing character of immigration to America. Occasionally these two conditions were simultaneous, as was the case in the latter half of the nineteenth century when immigrants from Bismarck's militarized Germany traveled with religious whose apostolate in their homeland had been cut off by the Kulturkampf, particularly by the Falk Ordinance of 1876. Of the thirty-eight German-founded communities now in the United States, thirty had sunk their roots deep in American soil before the beginning of the century.

There has been relatively little immigration directly from France (the majority of Americans of French descent are such because of Napoleon's sale of New Orleans, the accession of French Northwest Territory, or through later immigration from Canada) but twenty-eight French congregations came to the United States after the Third Republic passed the Law of Associations, July 1, 1901.

The wave of Italian and Slavic immigration which occurred in the late nineteenth and early twentieth centuries is reflected in the thirty-one Italian foundations and the six from Poland that established their convents here during that period. Twentieth-century religious persecutions in Mexico and Russia are reflected in the fact that all six of the Mexican foundations, and all eleven of the communities which· began in countries now behind the Iron Curtain (Russia, Lithuania, Hungary, Czechoslovakia), came to the United States during this century.

Encouraging though the increase in religious was, there were never enough to go around, and many bishops found themselves imitating Father Jean Harper, founder of the Sisters of the Assumption of the Blessed Virgin Mary, who said, "We cannot obtain nuns? Then, let us make some!" Fifty-seven American foundations in the nineteenth century and forty-four in the twentieth century came into being to fill the increasing needs of a pluralistic and urbanized society.[17]

The works of these active communities fall into three main divisions, as might be expected, with education the major apostolate of 256, nursing of 164, and social service of 64. This three-track breakdown, however, does not give any indication of the diversified activities which have branched out from the original simple trunk, or of the growing number of individual religious who have been given special assignments by their communities in rapidly widening apostolic areas. For example, those congregations which list education as their apostolate are engaged not only in teaching in elementary, secondary schools, and on college campuses, but have permitted sisters to teach in Catholic and state universities (several are visiting professors in non-

Catholic theological seminaries), and to serve full or part
time in Newman centers. They conduct orphanages, schools
for the blind, the deaf, the emotionally disturbed, mentally
retarded, and for children with cerebral palsy. They teach
on Indian reservations, conduct interracial forums, direct
local Operation Head Start activities, are officially involved
in the Council for Interracial Justice, and open their schools
in the summer to special groups such as Operation Upward
Bound. They are engaged in catechetical work both in
teaching CCD courses to teen-agers and adults, and as instructors of the children in the classes themselves. They staff
summer day camps as well as resident summer camps, and
conduct religious correspondence schools. Christian art
centers are a major concern of twenty one congregations;
three list the establishing of neighborhood libraries as a
major apostolic effort, and nine consider communication—
publishing, radio, cinema, TV—their chief concern. The
founding and training of native sisterhoods in foreign lands
is the crowning apostolic work of seven American congregations.

Communities which listed nursing as their major activity
have equally diversified outlets for their works of mercy. In
addition to hospitals and schools of nursing several have
collaborated with state institutions and are on state nursing
or technical staffs. Homes for the aged, for the mentally ill,
for unwed mothers, and for foundlings are familiar fields of
their dedication, as are their homes for the blind, for crip-
pled children, for retired priests, and the home nursing in
which thirty communities are engaged. Less well known to
the general public, perhaps, are the twelve which train
young women to be doctors for the foreign missions, or the
fourteen which prepare their members to do specialized
nursing and laboratory work in the leprosaria of the world.
There are two congregations whose members have laboratory
research as an apostolate, and one, the Sisters of Jesus
Crucified, conducts cytology laboratories for the early de-
tection of cancer, a corporal work of mercy of which Mother
Rose Hawthorne would thoroughly approve.

The specific works of the social service congregations are

less easily categorized. Many of their services are carried on in collaboration with the other two groups as well as with already established community organizations. They do have distinctive activities, however, such as parish visiting and taking of the parish census, management of homes for working girls, and travelers. One community includes a diversified service to immigrants, meeting them at their arrival, contacting sponsors and arranging for further travel to destination, assisting in the inevitable difficulties of adjustment, and introducing the newcomers to the various civil, religious, and educational organizations in the area. They visit prisoners, serve on parole boards, conduct child care centers, and staff psychological referral agencies. Three communities work in factories and fifty-one have lay retreat houses. The varied activities of the 121 congregations with sisters in the foreign mission field could not possibly be tabulated. As one sister, recently returned from South America, commented, "The one rule of the missions is flexibility. The need dictates the work, and what is required of the missionary here is the eye to see, the skilled hand to do, and the heart to understand and respect the dignity of the poor who are being served."

There are, of course, scores of apostolates in which individual religious are engaged with the approval and cooperation of their congregations. Some are better known than others, but there are any number serving on various state and national committees, or working full or part time with the National Catholic Education Association, National Catholic Council for Interracial Justice, and National Association for the Advancement of Colored People. This does not include the sister lawyer, the sister pilot, the sister member of the League of Women Voters.

There are, of course, many areas in which the American nun has not been sufficiently involved. She herself is the first to admit this, but it is equally obvious that many religious have been quietly adapting to the contemporary world for the past several decades. Those who have not done so sufficiently are being urged by the decree on appropriate renovation of religious life to engage upon a self-study to decide what areas of their apostolate may need updating.

In the apostolate of the future some of the works currently engaged upon will remain constant. At a conference held in New York in October 1966, Dr. Herman Kahn, director of the Hudson Institute, pointed out that women are finding it easier than men to make the necessary adjustments to a world changing at an accelerating rate, probably because fields that have traditionally been the province of women, such as education and the kinds of "help" occupations involved in poverty programs, are still primarily theirs. In these areas, as urbanization and socio-economic interdependence bring people closer together physically, and farther apart emotionally, religious women will have an important role as "facilitators of person-to-person contact."

Religious women in the post-conciliar world, involved in an examination of her past, is faced with the problems of adjustment to a challenging future. In charting that future, congregations of religious women must make sure to steer clear of what Jung calls the twin neuroses, one of which canonizes the past, and the other of which worships the future. They must realize that whatever changes are made must of their nature be temporary, for as Adolfs has pointed out, *metanoia* is not a momentary, once-for-all occurrence, but a continuous process of growth in believing. They will recall that true reform implies an appeal from a less perfect to a more perfect tradition, a going back to the sources, to a spirituality which does not force a choice between an interior and a social tendency, but which in all its authentic forms will share in both, in their extraordinary variety.

THREE

Focus of Change In Religious Life

Early during the first session of Vatican II a rumor filtered out of Rome which, like all rumors, caused considerable discussion both among those who would have been directly concerned and those less personally involved. The whisper was that the Council fathers with the approval of the Holy Father intended to dissolve all religious congregations and to establish guidelines for the establishment of lay groups of both men and women who would, under the direction of the hierarchy in each country, take over the corporal and spiritual works of mercy now being done by active religious. There were dark hints of what the future might bring; the relevancy of the nun in the twentieth-century world was hotly debated, and the prophets of doom cited as parallel the dissolution of medieval anchorholds.

Chapter VI of the *Dogmatic Constitution on the Church,* even before the *Decree on the Appropriate Renewal of Religious Life* made it clear that whatever the source of the rumor, the considered decision of Vatican II did not envision the end of religious life but its deepening. Nor, apparently, was this the result of a refusal to cope with the difficulties involved in the dissolution of centuries-old establishments. The decree on the missionary activity of the Church explicitly states that "right from the planting stage of the Church, the religious life should be carefully fostered. This not only confers precious and absolutely necessary as-

sistance on missionary activity, but, by a more inward
consecration made to God in the Church, it also luminously
manifests and signifies the inner nature of the Christian
calling" (*Ad gentes,* #18).

Clearly in making its recommendations the Council was
of Mortimer Adler's opinion that "to constitute a genuine
advance, progress must conserve whatever was good or true
in the old, and transform it by the addition of the new,
resulting in a greater good. . . ." [1]

Adjustment to the current need has been a historical factor
in the growth of religious congregations. When immigrant
nuns from Europe saw that the cloistered isolation of their
nineteenth-century convents would not serve the Church in
the New World, they took steps to have this mitigated, some
within the first decade after their arrival. The monastic tradition which restricted educational efforts to the teaching
of little girls, and even these within the walls of the convent
home, gave way to the practical requirements of the newly
established parochial school system advocated by the American bishops, in which boys, even of high school age, were
enrolled. Sister nurses, with Our Lady's visit to Elizabeth as
precedent, sought and obtained permission from the Holy
See to assist at deliveries and to take care of sick of both
sexes in the hospitals mushrooming across the nation.
Cardinal Suenens' *The Nun in the Modern World* found the
receptive reading public it did, both because the nun was
already engaged in weighing the relative value of her
apostolic works, and because she felt that in many cases the
adjustments which her individual congregation had made
to the peculiar needs of the contemporary world were perhaps too few and too limited in their scope. There was a
restlessness generated by the climate of the post-war generation's eagerness to become involved in the manifold apostolic functions which cried for immediate attention, and
from the juridical restrictions which many felt prevented
their accomplishment.

Some of the criticism which saw the religious woman as
one isolated from the mainstream of American life was
justified; a good deal of it, however, has been based upon

inadequate or inaccurate information. Although the impetus for "appropriate renovation" has been specifically generated by Vatican II, and all congregations are currently involved in self-examination and experimentation for the ultimate revision of rules and customs, much quietly achieved progress and adjustment has already taken place.

In my own congregation, whose unilateral dedication has been educational since its foundation in the sixteenth century, the past decade has seen an enlarging of the definition of that broad term so that at the 1966 inter-provincial education meeting at Mequon, Wisconsin, a survey revealed that in addition to formal teaching at all levels, members of the community in the United States are engaged in activities other than traditional teaching, including work in Newman centers, catechetical institutes, diocesan ccd boards, Catholic Charities research committees, lay-teacher training groups, and seminary faculties.

The sisters of many of our provinces have "come nearer to the poor" by their work in Head Start and Poverty programs, reading centers, adult education groups, summer camps, educational TV programs, and schools for the handicapped. One sister taught in the first Outdoor Education Program set up under Title I of the ESEA at Marshfield High School Forest. Two taught in the Go-Go program in Detroit —an educational and cultural experiment for the underprivileged. A sister is serving on the Governor's Committee of Recommendations for Education in Louisiana; several are on the faculties of secular universities.

One hundred ninety-seven American missionary ssNDs are giving dedicated service in Brazil, Bolivia, Peru, Colombia, Chile, Guam, Japan, Okinawa, Puerto Rico, Guatemala; and in our newest mission in Paraguay, sisters engage in catechetical work, adult education, census taking, and the operation of a health clinic (*Inter-Provincial News Letter* of the School Sisters of Notre Dame, XXXVII, October 1966, p. 22).

Other congregations have similarly expanded the scope of their service even before the convening of the general chapter designed to make the major changes inherent in the recommendations of the Council. Sister M. Angelica Seng reports on Chicago's Urban Apostolate of the Sisters, which has a threefold program of education whereby the sisters become aware of the many dimensions of the work of the Church and the needs of human society; of communication whereby the sisters learn from the thinking, the successes, and the failures of others, and are encouraged and strengthened by them; and of action whereby the sisters, as a result of study and planning, take appropriate steps to aid in the solution of the problems of the people of the inner city.[2] The Cabrini program of the School Sisters of St. Francis begun in 1962; Rendu House, the apartment leased by the Daughters of Charity for closer contact between the residents in a Chicago Housing Authority high-rise building; the adult evening basic education courses given by the sisters of the Institute of the Blessed Virgin Mary in the Woodlawn area of Chicago; the participation of sisters in the migrant workers' as well as in inter-racial and anti-war demonstrations across the nation are evidence that all cloisters are not closed and that all religious are not cozily unconscious of world problems.

There is, however, validity in the accusation that there is a tendency for conventual life to become formalized and tradition-ridden. Some congregations have been noticeably slow in internal adaptation to the contemporary spiritual needs of their own members and the apostolic scriptural-liturgical training of the young women who enter their ranks. Reluctance to make major changes without mature deliberation may be justified, but reluctance to change because of smug satisfaction or a blind unawareness of contemporary needs is a betrayal of the very purpose for which active religious congregations exist.

Whether we will or not, the world is changing rapidly, and where congregations do not adjust to the accelerated tempo, the gap between them and those they would serve will inevitably become wider and more impassible.

It is not necessary to agree with the social worker who prophesied in a recent issue of the New York *Times* that the nun of tomorrow will do her best work in the bar. I find it a little hard to envision a bartender willing to have a non-drinking customer occupying space, and even harder to see how I, at least, would be capable of any apostolic work were I to join the crowd, but that is a personal reflection. The point I am making is that it is not necessary to accept the prophet of the fluid phenomenon, but it is difficult not to see the need of widening the horizons of apostolic endeavor.

There are vast areas of contemporary life where the nun has had no impact, and where with considerably less than a drastic change of her life pattern she might easily enter. Even within the established works in which she is now engaged there are opportunities she has not utilized. The imaginative individuals who have been courageous enough to see the potential in strange though related roles have been welcomed.

Sister Mary Immaculate, executive secretary-treasurer of the national Catholic theater conference and promoter of the John F. Kennedy Center for the Performing Arts is one of the most influential figures in American theater. On a friendly basis with some of Broadway's brightest luminaries she is also keenly aware of her responsibility as a witness for Christ. "The more a man thinks of God, the more likely he is to be saved," she remarked to an interviewer. "My presence reminds them of God. I make sure it does." Her friends comment that her stability and charity are legend in the topsy-turvy world of show business.[3] Once when she was asked why she bothered talking with a man whose moral character was "at the bottom of my list," as the questioner put it, she replied, "My list doesn't have a bottom. Neither did Christ's."

Like Sister Mary Immaculate, Sister Corita of Immaculate Heart College, Los Angeles, whose seriographs have made her famous in art circles around the world, and Sister Mary Remy, SSND, winner of the American Architects' award in 1967, whose associations with the sophisticated world of the artist are well established, have done much to destroy some of the well-nurtured stereotypes of the nun as medieval, quaint, or cute.

These sisters, as well as the countless others whose professional competence in specialized areas has earned them the respect of their secular peers, have done much to destroy the image of the nun which the entertainment world, unfortunately, has helped to create. One has only to recall the vulgar sentimentality of *The Bells of St. Mary's,* the sweet mediocrity of *For Heaven's Sake, Mr. Allison,* the absence of any real religious feeling in *The Nun's Story,* or the schmalz with decorative song and dance of *The Singing Nun.* Convents do have a good deal of music, liturgical and otherwise, but even in the most choral-minded congregation, life is considerably more complex than three-part harmonizing. Not all religious women are young, beautiful, and talented, but neither are they either old and crotchety or old and wise.

Not all teaching sisters are highly educated specialists, but by the law of averages, neither are all secular educators; and my observation in the various professional organizations of which I am a member has led me to conclude that, proportionally, there are as many if not more graduate degrees in the average elementary or secondary school taught by nuns as in the nearby public school; there are as many dynamic and gifted teachers, as many productive scholars. Professional preparation before engaging in the works of the congregation may be a comparatively recent part of a sister's training, the result in part, at least, of the Sister Formation Conference, but the records of America's universities show a respectable number of Ph.D.s earned by American sisters a half century ago. As Americans in general and American Catholics in particular have become more professionally orientated the American nun has become a familiar figure on campuses across the nation. Her absence at large and famous universities until quite recently sprang as much from the proscriptions of the hierarchy, which feared the scandal her presence there might give the lay Catholic who was being urged to attend Catholic colleges, as from any doubt of her ability to achieve a satisfactory standard of performance, or any fear of exposing her to the threats of a secular civilization.

All of this is not meant to imply that the renewal recommended by the Council is not necessary, but to point out that the process of updating had already begun. Pope Pius XII urged modification of the religious habit and encouraged major superiors to give adequate and professional training to their sisters, and even urged some of the cloistered congregations in Italy to become actively engaged in apostolic work.

All of this change has as its fixed and avowed purpose the bringing of the nun into closer relationship with those she serves that she may become a more relevant factor in giving Christ's Gospel to all men. All congregations had very real relevance to their times when they were founded; there is nothing revolutionary, then, in making them equally so today, although it may take revolutionary soul searching to discover just where change is needed, in the local situation, for a particular congregation. Numerous interlocking factors will need to be considered by each congregation individually, and St. Vincent de Paul's famous dictum that the "need creates the worker" may well be applied here.

Reform of tremendous proportion is taking place in the Church and in religious life. Since the changes under consideration will involve the lives of thousands it is no cause for wonder that religious themselves are eager to experiment, to weigh suggestions, and fear to have the important issues buried under trivia. Many of the points urged for consideration in both Catholic and secular periodicals appear to spring from too great concentration on the petty, and from too superficial a knowledge of the essence of religious life itself. I have been amused by the fulminations of lay advisers who would have religious women freed from the restrictions put upon their freedom by their local ordinaries, but who see no inconsistency in prescribing in areas where the bishop, prohibited by canon law from interfering in the internal life of the community, would fear to tread.

What is too frequently omitted in discussions on the updating of religious life is the fact that "religious life, charismatically given to the Church by Christ Himself, exists in the Church only as canonically submissive to her law," [4] and thus actually exists "only when it is discerned, judged, approved, controlled, supported, and criticized by hierarchical action, local or supreme, of which it can neither attempt nor desire to be free." [5] For active religious the apostolate can never be separated from the dedicated life, and although the manner of its mission may well be placed under scrutiny, the essential quality, the attempt to express through the vows in concentrated form the vocation to holiness of the entire Church, remains stable. Father Martelet points out that concern for *doing* what one judges to be most useful for Christ's kingdom will never replace the primordial importance of attaching oneself to Christ for what he *is* in himself. If this latter commitment is lacking, there will one day be an awakening to find oneself basically committed, but not for the sake of a person. Then comes the crisis in action, practices, spirit.[6] Religious life is first of all the choice of an end, and only secondly of a system of means.

Renovation of spirit for religious institutes, as for the Church herself, demands not that the structures be discarded but that they be re-examined, perhaps reconstituted so that they may safeguard the spiritual realities which are their justification. The vows which symbolize the total gift of self for love must be examined in the light of that objective, interpreted in terms of the triple good which they represent, and understood not as negative restrictions but as positive and explosive forces which like Dylan Thomas' "force that through the green fuse drives the flower/drives my green age."

As Father de Lubac has indicated,[7] Catholic spirituality has not to choose between an "interior" and a "social" tendency, but all its authentic forms in their extraordinary variety will share in both. A charity fully conscious of its own requirements does not neglect those most hidden tasks or hold in low esteem the so-called duties toward oneself, any more than it forgets justice.

The renovation of religious life depends today as in the past upon the Holy Spirit, so that the sister's temporal involvement may serve as a charism penetrating today's civilization.

FOUR

That Troublesome
Vow of Obedience

In a world which glorifies freedom and personal responsibility, it is inevitable that the vow of obedience should receive considerable criticism, that general misunderstanding both of its essence and nature as well as an exaggerated emphasis on the abuse of authority both historical and contemporary should result in serious questioning of the very authenticity of the vow. The Council fathers themselves wrestled with the problem of authority versus freedom, returning to it again and again in discussion and incorporating some specific interpretations in eleven of the sixteen Council documents.

There have been almost as many definitions of freedom as there have been men who defined it. One which recognizes the paradox of the moment, recognizing the fact that freedom today is threatened and is today itself a threat, is that given in the Declaration on Religious Freedom. The document urges everyone, especially those charged with the task of educating others, to do their utmost to form men who will respect the moral order and be obedient to lawful authority; it then goes on to recommend further that they form men, too, who will be lovers of true freedom—"men, in other words, who will come to decisions on their own judgment and in the light of truth, govern their activities with a sense of responsibility, and strive after what is true and right, willing always to join with others in cooperative

47

effort. Religious freedom, therefore, ought to have this further purpose and aim, namely, that men may come to act with greater responsibility in fulfilling their duties in community life." [1]

While a definition of freedom may seem at the opposite pole from a definition of the vow of obedience, any religious aware of the area covered by her vow and its implications would be willing to accept the above definition as a fairly accurate summary of the vow. In obedience she is not less free but more so, having made an initial choice which integrates her entire life, a decision which enables her "with greater responsibility" to fulfill the duties of her social commitment.

Like the other two vows, obedience is a profession of love, a living in and through love. The vow is made to God, but fulfilled in and through relationship with people; it is a public manifestation of communion, an acceptance of group decisions, expressed by the superior who, as Father Tillard expresses it, "is placed between two obediences: obedience to the call of the Lord to this individual, and obedience to the generous response of this individual and to his desire for the evangelical life." [2]

It is significant that Section 14 dealing with obedience in *Perfectae Caritatis* uses the word *service* or a synonym ten times, and that religious are encouraged to bring to the execution of commands and to the discharge of assignments entrusted to them the resources of their minds and wills, their gifts of nature and grace. It is a far cry from the frequently expressed accusation that obedience crushes initiative and stunts growth.

Obedience is not a surrender, but a sharing of responsibility. That both superiors and sisters in a given community have permitted this concept to become buried under the weight of tradition does not nullify the reality. Superiors exercise authority when their decisions are a reflection of the contributions of the community. The individual sister's obedience does not consist in submission but in co-operation, not in passivity but in an eager activity adapting itself to the changing circumstances of each day.

A few years ago, while the Council was still in session, I wrote an article on the troublesome vow of obedience which was printed in *The Critic*.[3] In considering this chapter I reread the article and discovered that what I said then is still my firm conviction. For this reason I have decided not to attempt to rephrase that conviction, but to incorporate it, as originally written, here. Either I have not changed in the past years, or my original belief is valid. I should like to think it is the latter, but whichever is the case, "Here I Stand."

Not too many years ago a young woman who decided to enter the convent was reasonably sure that, with the exception of her family and friends and those whom she would eventually serve in the apostolate, no one was interested in her. She might wear several yards of serge and starched linen as she traveled about, but for all the attention she drew, she might as well have been invisible. Although the sisters served in thousands of schools and orphanages, hospitals and homes for the aged, only statisticians were interested.

Even though the sister might be the twentieth-century mystery woman, she was, until recently, not newsworthy. Perhaps my own experience was unusual, but before my decision to enter religious life I had met just three nuns in print: a glamorous young woman, in a novel whose title I have forgotten, who inherited several million dollars the night before her final profession and was urged by her superior to go out and spend a few million before taking the vow of poverty; the sadly romantic heroine of *The White Sister;* and the authentic Carmelite, Thérèse of Lisieux, whose *Histoire d'une Ame* I tackled as supplementary reading in a French course.

Today, however, the nun like the layman has emerged, at least in the public consciousness. Her picture appears in *Life* and *Look* and *Time*. Hollywood has discovered her and both used and misused her. She has been written about in such unlikely periodicals as *Réalités* and *Harper's,* and she does some writing herself. Although admittedly there are times when she thinks nostalgically of the days when what she did with her life was her own business, she continues to answer the inevitable questions about her habit, her prayer life, her apostolate, and her vows.

Frequently these questions are not so much information seeking as they are check backs on information already gleaned. Last June, for instance, I had dinner with the staff of a New York mental hospital where I had been invited to speak. It was a pleasantly relaxed dinner party, and the conversation was casual. But before we had finished the first course it had veered to religious life. Those within talking range (none of whom shared my faith) sought confirmation for facts they had drawn from Monica Baldwin's little saga, or *The Nun's Story,* or from Ed Sullivan's featuring of Soeur Marie de Sourire. All were courteously curious and surprisingly perceptive.

One young doctor asked whether the report he had heard that nuns in America were leaving the convent in great numbers was true. When I answered that I did not have the statistics, but if the numbers in all communities matched those of my own, I suspected the report might be exaggerated, he shot a second question: "What in your opinion is the most difficult aspect of religious life today?"

I have been reading, too, and matching what I have read against experience, so I was able to come right back with the answer to that one. "Obedience," I said.

He nodded thoughtfully, and then added, "That makes sense; the Pepsi generation has grown up in a pretty permissive atmosphere." The table agreed, and the talk moved into more generalized channels, leaving me to reflect on the ease with which these professional people, whose own work is of necessity organized on a structure of concentric authority, accepted the natural aspects of obedience.

The very complexity of contemporary society requires most men to submit to regulations which they did not initiate and, in many cases, for which they did not vote. A century and a half ago an American deciding to travel to a neighboring town had only to harness his horse and gallop off. His progress might be conditioned by the weather, by Indians or bandits, but other than these accidental deterrents his trips were his own business.

Today's traveler, if he drives his own car, will have to have that car licensed and himself licensed as its driver. He will roll along established highways to whose upkeep he has contributed through taxes; he will keep to the right side of the road and within official speed limits. He will respond to stop-and-go lights, and will normally not consider his personal rights violated by any of these traffic regulations. If he elects to use public transportation, train, bus, or plane, he will make reservations in advance to assure himself a seat, and will have to adjust his travel time to the schedule set up by some board totally ignorant of him and his particular needs or convenience.

This type of submission to an external force does not, of course, have any relationship to religious obedience, but a good many of the regulations within a religious community necessarily grow out of a similar need to co-ordinate activities toward a common goal. These matters do not constitute the matter of the vow, although the virtue of obedience as well as the simple demands of courtesy may bind a religious to conformity. Strangely enough, much of the recent debate about religious obedience is concerned with these organizational details of community life.

During the past summer I have been struck by the similarity between the structure of religious communities and of the two educational organizations with which I have been privileged to work: The Advanced Placement Examination Readings, and the Wisconsin English-Language-Arts Curriculum Workshop. Both groups had invited specialists to serve; both groups had divided these specialists into subcommittees under a leader, and both had a staff of experts in the discipline who directed and channeled the work to be done and made final judgments in controversial areas. It was the rational method for achieving the goals we all shared.

Religious obedience differs essentially from this acceptance of authority upon which all community life, secular or religious, depends, as well as from the natural obedience of childhood to which the New York doctor referred. A guest at one of our profession ceremonies said recently, "That vow of obedience is the one that throws me. I couldn't stand having anyone tell me what to do." I suspect that young woman has a clearer concept of what the vow of obedience entails than the psychiatrist who associated it with un-questioning acceptance of authority, although she, too, has a blind spot that prevents her seeing the spiritual freedom achieved through the vow.

There is no denying the fact that authority and obedience are pejorative words to many people, or that freedom and personal responsibility are important concepts in the *aggiornamento* toward which the Church is moving. There is a valuable bulk of literature in these areas by experts in the fields of theology, philosophy, psychology, and sociology. There is also an increasing amount of non-professional writing which seems less concerned with clarifying issues than with stimulating letters to the editor—writing that too frequently draws large generalizations from particular in-stances and creates semantic problems that lead the discus-sion off into the brushwood.

For example, a highly intelligent friend of mine recently brought up the truism that no one could dispense me from my own conscience, and no superior could command me to do anything of which my conscience disapproved. He was right, of course, on both counts, and I couldn't agree with him more. Our disagreement grew out of his conviction that the vow of obedience obliged me to both under the name of blind obedience. I quoted my vow formula, by which I promised God obedience, "according to the rule of the congregation of the School Sisters of Notre Dame," and from my rule, based upon the code of canon law for religious which explicitly limits the authority of the superior to that "which is permissible"—a rule which restricts her more than it binds me, since it places boundaries upon her authority, limiting it not only to conformity with the Commandments, but even to the specific rule and constitutions, each of which has the approval of the Church.

He was not convinced. "You can't tell me you've never been given an assignment you didn't think was silly," he insisted. And we were off on another road, for a silly assign-

ment may be truly silly, or only seem such. In either case it
is a question of intellectual agreement, not of moral issue.
Genius is not required of a superior any more than it is of
the rest of us, and she will make mistakes. A nun with whom
I was living once told me she confessed her inability to overcome the feeling that she was more intelligent than her
superior and received the amused comment, "Stop torturing
yourself, Sister. You probably are."

To those who shout gleefully, "That's what I mean. You
don't have an opportunity to develop to your full potential,"
my answer is, "Who does?" The astronauts are carefully
selected for their ability to respond intelligently and immediately to an emergency, but they are briefed and de-
briefed, and follow directions from Gemini control scrupu-
lously. Unscheduled ham sandwiches are not looked upon
with favor!

As a matter of fact, the majority of religious superiors I
have met and lived with are well aware that they are not
specialists in all fields. Certainly the chemistry teacher
knows more in her area than her principal, unless the latter
also has a degree in science. The apostolic works of the
church require specialists, and communities are working full
time at providing them. Comparatively few religious women
would have had the time and opportunity to achieve parallel
professional excellence had they remained in the world.

A novice may receive more guidance than she appreciates,
but so does the novice in any field. I recall objecting when
I was a young professed sister that some school regulation
seemed petty. A companion commented wryly, "If it is petty,
why are you making such a fuss about it?"

A mature religious in twentieth-century America is rarely
restricted in the performance of her professional duties. The
assignment ordinarily carries with it the parallel permission
to make the decisions essential for its successful completion.
If these decisions necessitate requisitioning of supplies or
travel expenses, the religious woman will ask "permission,"
while the lay person in a similar position will write out an
order slip.

It would be psychologically and historically naïve to ignore the fact that religious life has not at all times or in all places given sufficient recognition to individual ability, or presented adequate opportunity for initiative, nor does it in all American convents today. Some customs might well be changed, and the Conference of Major Superiors of Women, one of the most "collegial" organizations in America, through open discussions has encouraged communities to take a long look at their customs and century-old traditions, to evaluate, discuss, and perhaps drop those which appear unessential, anachronistic, or incompatible with the American temperament. Give us time. After all, men have not yet dropped the obsolete buttons on their coat sleeves that were once functional aids in keeping their lace cuffs out of the gravy.

Since the appearance of Cardinal Suenens' *The Nun in the World,* sisters engaged in the active apostolate have been giving considerable thought to the works in which they are engaged. I have read with interest, and sometimes, I confess, a bit of irritation, articles dealing with the question —articles which imply that religious teachers and nurses are nearly unanimous in the conviction that their work is outdated and it is only their vow of obedience and the superior's lack of contact with the modern world that keeps the community bound to this work instead of allowing it to move out into the total commitment of social work, full-time catechetical work, Newman centers, interracial councils, foreign missions, or any other "apostolic" area. As a member of a congregation that has slowly and soberly over the past twenty years become involved in additional works within the framework of our Constitution (which has teaching as its major objective), I feel justified in denying both the unanimity of the attitude and the relevance of the vow of obedience in the discussion.

I have great admiration for the sisters of our community currently opening a religious teaching center, and for those working in the already established centers, as well as for those whose departure ceremonies we of the Mequon province attend each year before they leave for the missions in Guam or South America. I am impressed with the enthusiasm and dedication of those working in underprivileged areas, or who have opened neighborhood libraries, or who teach in state universities and serve as advisers to their Newman clubs. But when I express the wish that we could do more of this sort of thing, it is always for other sisters I see engaged in work for which I know I have neither competence nor training. Obedience places us all where our capabilities can best be used; both they and I have been given assignments which are apostolic in essence.

But *all* of this is tangential to the heart of the matter: that vow of obedience. I have dwelt on these fringe areas at such length simply because so much criticism of religious life and of obedience in recent years has focused on them. The religious, as someone has pointed out, is like the Levite in the Old Testament, a witness to the world that all men belong to God. The sister pronounces her vows "in the presence of the convent community," but she makes them to God alone. Obedience is the complete and irrevocable acceptance of the will of God in the circumstances and situations in which the community life she has freely chosen shall place her, "sin alone excepted." It is a gift of self, born of love of God and fulfilled daily. There is a direct relationship between a sister's recognition that her personal fulfillment as a woman lies not in inert acceptance of the passive will of God, but in personal, dynamic spending of her gifts, talents, and time in his service through the vow by which her offering is concretized. As Father Elio Gambari has pointed out in Spiritual Institutes to Formation personnel, "Obedience is a fecund vow; the works of religious in the world are the fruit of that obedience." It is a continual choice of the will of God, a progressive correspondence with the Holy Spirit, and for each religious it is an opportunity given daily to express visibly in deeds the consecration of her heart. It is a freely chosen pattern of life, as marriage is a freely chosen pattern of life, and the religious, like the wife, achieves her own sanctity and contributes to that of others within its framework.

The rules, constitutions, and customs of each religious community are approved by the Church, and the sister who takes vows has been given every opportunity to become acquainted with these and to live according to them during the novitiate. That she cannot know or anticipate the specific areas in which they will function is normal to the human situation. The bride makes her promise: ". . . from this day forward, for better, for worse; for richer, for poorer; in sickness and in health, till death do us part," not knowing which of the alternatives will predominate in her life. The sister who accepts the common mode of religious life in imitation of the obedience of Christ may not foresee, when she pronounces her vows, the specific areas of her apostolate or the superiors who will assign it, but she accepts her unknown future in faith and with love as does the bride.

As Karl Rahner says, "If we can enter in Christ's obedience, even partially, then we will begin to understand that the saints who could obey without getting angry or bitter, who were dumb enough to obey when commanded, could tumble into the most holy life of God with this silent obedience of theirs—an obedience brought into this world by the Incarnate Son of God." [4]

FIVE

"Having Nothing We Possess All Things"— The Vow of Poverty

The vow of poverty presents as many problems to the uninitiated onlooker as the vow of obedience, and a good deal of the confusion results from a semantic block. For one thing, Americans are against poverty on principle; we even have a government-financed war on poverty, and it is the rare grade-school child who has not been taught that "early to bed, early to rise makes a man healthy, wealthy, and wise." Poverty, to the average man, is defined in terms of the social reality—the state of the poor who have little or no means of support. If he envisions a dedication to voluntary poverty at all, it is usually the figure of Gandhi, the great, poor man of India, whose deathbed possessions would not cover a small table top, that comes to mind.

Poverty as professed by the religious shares, theoretically at least, some of the aspects of both of these examples, but differs essentially from both. This, obviously, complicates its meaning further, as does the juridical distinction between the obligations arising from the vow of poverty and the ascetical implications of the virtue. By the vow, the sister freely offers God all her property, as well as the right to control any property or income she may acquire later, either through inheritance or through her personal activity. The vow presumes that the religious has accepted Christ's invitation to leave all things and to follow him who had not where to lay his head. There was a significant symbolism in

57

the venerable if outmoded use of the plural instead of the singular possessive. Since all things are held in common, and even those articles which are given a religious for her exclusive use are given as aids to an apostolic assignment, they are truly "ours," not mine. Novices, at times, have been so intrigued by the novelty of the expression as to perpetrate such verbal atrocities as "our toothbrush," or the physiologically impossible "our feet," but the communal pronoun remains a linguistic reminder of the individual commitment.

That the renovation of religious life recommended by Vatican II does not include a lessening of the vow of poverty is clearly indicated in the provision by which "religious communities can allow their members to renounce any inheritance which they have acquired or are due to acquire." [1] Until the promulgation of this decree, renunciation of inheritance had been a distinguishing mark of final and solemn vows as distinguished from temporary and simple vows. [2]

The taking of the vow, however, is not in itself the objective toward which a religious is aiming. It is only the means by which the greater good, the virtue of poverty, or to use the phrase with connotative value for the contemporary American, the virtue of *detachment,* may be acquired. Sister Madeleva, csc, called it the relaxed grasp, the ability to use all things with appreciation but without the squirrel's need to hide them away for personal, exclusive use later. This is, of course, the difficulty.

As the directress of our novitiate pointed out, all of us are born with fingers curled inward, and one of the first instinctive acts of the newborn baby is to grasp tightly whatever touches the small palm. With the exception of certain dramatic lovers of Lady Poverty such as St. Francis and St. Clare, or the twentieth-century Charles de Foucauld, most men find it a lifetime task to loosen the acquisitive fist. It is toward this flexibility that both virtue and vow of poverty tend, and with a completely spiritual end in view, a close imitation in love of the poor Christ.

It is as important for the lay Catholic to understand as it is for the sister herself that she does not give up material

things because they are bad. On the contrary, she gives them
to God just because they are good and are, therefore, worthy
to be gifts. C. S. Lewis points out in *Screwtape Letters* that
it is one of the frustrations of the devil that he has not been
able to create a single sin which is not a perverted use of one
of the good gifts God has given man. Satan did not create
the diamonds, or jewels, or uranium, or oil for which men
steal and murder and wage war. It is the Puritan or
Jansenist who suspects beauty, who judges a thing to be evil
precisely because it is pleasant. Religious poverty is not the
contemporary version of the ancient philosopher's scorn of
material goods. Father Danielou has pointed out that
"religious poverty needs to be defined essentially in its
relation to God, and not, first of all, in its relation to
material goods." 3

We are at work to establish the kingdom of God here, as
far as we can, which means that the realities of this world
must be transfigured, but first we must, so to speak, turn
them around. As Father Régamey indicates, "Our point of
view is divine, our object is divine, but our material is the
realities of this world." 4

It is a source of some satisfaction to the confused Christian
to note that even the evangelists seem to have had some
difficulty in deciding exactly what comprised· evangelical
poverty. St. Matthew in his reporting of the Beatitudes
quotes Christ as saying, "Blessed are the poor in spirit; the
kingdom of heaven is theirs" (Mt 5:3), but St. Luke's account says, "Blessed are you who are poor; the kingdom of
God is yours." (Lk 6:20) It does not take a linguist to point
out that the two versions differ in meaning significantly.
Exegetes have been explaining the distinction for centuries.
While no one will argue the accuracy of those who point out
that a rich man who is not attached to his riches may be
more possessed of the true spirit of poverty than the poor
man who envies him, I am reminded of a student who
wondered whether those who so glibly pointed out the
superiority of spiritual poverty felt the same way when they
were hungry. Père Chevrier's wry comment that "those who

have only interior poverty run the risk of having none at all," is sharp comment on this danger.

And it is precisely in this area that religious today may fail to give witness and may even give scandal. Even unbelievers recognize the poverty of Christ and expect to see that poverty reflected in those who profess themselves his followers.

The incompatibility of the professed poverty of the individual religious and the communal wealth of the congregation may well become a scandal. William Langland and Geoffrey Chaucer record their cynical appraisal of the fifteenth-century world's religious mendicant whose sleek appearance betrays a life of comfort lived amid the pleasant possessions of the monastery. Expanding physical plants built to take care of the needs of an increased professional commitment have led the contemporary religious into what appears to be a similar contradiction: a professed poverty lived in institutional security. Sister Bertrande Meyers [5] has pointed out the inherent incongruity in corporate wealth and meaningful personal poverty. Many religious themselves wonder about the reality of their poverty in the face of facts that the geography of world hunger has revealed. With 30 million people [6] dying annually of starvation and undernourishment her own life of evangelical poverty seems far removed in spirit and fact from the degrading pauperism, destitution, and hunger in which more than one third of the world's inhabitants live. The Council fathers were aware of this dichotomy and the decree *Perfectae Caritatis* (#13) states clearly that "religious poverty requires more than limiting the use of possessions to the consent of superiors; members of a community ought to be poor in both fact and spirit, and have their treasure in heaven."

This is complicated in today's world, however, by the sophisticated needs of contemporary professionalism which demand advanced preliminary training, an educational preparation which puts an incredible financial drain upon a congregation. The training of the "non-productive" young sisters, as well as the care of the increasing number of aged sisters, requires buildings of a size which would undoubtedly startle the indigent founders of an earlier generation. The decree (#13) takes today's needs into consideration in saying that "to the degree that their rules and constitutions permit, religious communities can rightly possess whatever is necessary for their temporal life and their mission. Still, let them avoid every appearance of luxury, or excessive wealth, and accumulation of possessions."

It is with the recommendations of the last sentence that American religious are concerned, and to which they are giving attention. Functional buildings whose purpose is service are recognized for what they are. It is the use of luxury materials and unnecessary large grounds that resemble estates of European nobility which are inconsistent with the profession of poverty and with the works of the apostolate. But even here prudent evaluation of purpose is not necessarily to be interpreted as justification of an all-too-obvious evil. There may well be situations in which extensive grounds are necessary that the work of the institute may be effectively achieved. No one would accuse Dorothy Day of a lack of understanding of poverty, yet she has some wry comments to make about visitors to the Catholic Worker farms who are distressed by the painstakingly kept gardens, the neatly laid-out paths, and who are blind to the very real evidence of want. There is, however, a growing recognition of the issue involved in communal witness to poverty, and the future may well see congregations relinquishing the ownership of large institutions, serving instead as employees in what was originally corporate religious property.

Decisions such as these which involve the entire congregation will have to be worked out by the major superiors meeting with their councilors in general chapters. The reflective renewal of the individual religious' dedication to her vow, however, need not wait for any such formal gathering. A recognition of the ramifications of evangelical poverty, "each religious should regard himself as subject to the common law of labor," [7] indifference to the quality of clothes, refusal to accumulate superfluities, and what Father Häring calls the obligation to be really free from all kinds of greed and to take care that our witness to the eschatological realities be credible to men are immediate possibilities. The nun may need go no farther than her desk where she has two fountain pens—one of which may be needed by a child or a colleague.

It is the experience of many that the really destitute are first to recognize the detached dedication in the nun. The frequency with which those whom John Cogley calls the "Brothers of the Open Palm" approach the nun to ask for alms is witness of this fact. They do not anticipate rebuff, for they instinctively expect the sister will respect their dignity even when the coin with which she responds to their appeal is a small one. On more than one occasion I have had the moving experience of being stopped by one whose threadbare clothes and haggard appearance marked him as one of Christ's needy, who, after fumbling in a coat pocket, produced a pitiful handful of pennies which he offered with the request that I give it to the poor. It was a tribute, not only to his own greatness of heart, but to all the sisters whose generosity had convinced him that giving was a part of their lives. The Little Sisters of the Poor continue to inspire the generous, for it is no secret that whatever is received goes directly to the old whom they so lovingly serve.

For many religious, however, what constitutes poverty for the laity—worry over job security, the pile up of unexpected expenses, and concern for the well-being and education of a growing family—does not exist. For all except superiors, for whom the balancing of income against incoming bills may be as difficult a problem as for the father of a family, the commitment to poverty is expressed in dependence upon the community for necessities of human living, a willingness to share as well as to work energetically in the particular apostolate of the institute, and a refusal to be possessed by things.

The decree (#14) specifically calls on religious communities to identify with the poor: "Let them willingly contribute something from their own resources to the other needs of the Church, and to the support of the poor, whom religious should love with the tenderness of Christ." Details of this increased donating must be worked out within particular congregations, but there are ways by which individual religious can anticipate the decisions of their communities. B. M. Chevignard insists, "I am a disciple of Christ only if, in total truth, I have a friend, I have friends, among the poor." [8] It is difficult to conceive of a work in which the nun is engaged which would not provide opportunities for this very real involvement. The Constitutions of the School Sisters of Notre Dame point out that the poor are not only those lacking worldly goods. In our affluent society some of us may have limited opportunities for contact with these, but they may be those who lack talent or good will, and within this broadened concept there are multiple opportunities for service to the underprivileged. While the scandal of America's "Appalachias" calls for community witness, we dare not neglect these others whose need is less obvious, but who also have souls for whom Christ died. It may even be possible to bring those whose poverty is not material into association with the congregation in its work for the others. Projects like Detroit's Commitment, Equality, Scope, Head Start, Identity, Neighborhood Youth Corps, Fresh Start have increasing need for dedicated personnel, on either a full-time or part-time basis. Colleges and high schools have included the training of students in these works as part of their educational program, and the enthusiasm and generous self-sacrifice of these young people working with the sisters is contagious. Schools which are most involved in service for others find that it is the students with the finest academic records who are most eager to become involved. In my own college, Spanish students, for the past several years under the direction of an enthusiastic young nun, have been giving more time than any of us would have prophesied to the Spanish-speaking Center in Milwaukee's inner city, and summer after summer go blithely off to Mexico as participants in CICOP's program of service. Approximately one third of the students at Immaculate Heart College in Los Angeles contribute time and talent to educational projects in Watts. In fact, I would venture to guess that there are few Catholic schools whose faculty and students are not actively involved in some direct service of this nature, and the future will see more rather than less of this.

But there are other unexplored areas to which nuns might offer themselves, if only on a part-time basis. Some communities are already traveling with migrant workers during the summer, setting up vacation schools, catechetical centers, even job stations where contacts for more permanent work opportunities are made. But the need here far surpasses the numbers engaged in alleviating it, probably because the plight of the migrant worker is less publicized than that of the unionized laborers. Social education is a correlative factor not only in the training of the young nun, but also of those whose local or parochial apostolate has so occupied them as to keep them unaware of the appalling social inequities in our affluent society.

The traveling workshop of the Catholic Interracial Council includes as part of its program the showing of two films, one of which is NBC's "Harvest of Shame," dealing with the desperate subhuman situation of the thousands of migrant workers in the United States. It has been a sobering and fruitful experience for the many who have viewed it. A recognition of what Thomas Merton calls the reality of poverty, and a realization that "to make a vow of poverty and never go without anything, never have to need something without getting it, is to try to mock the living God," [9] demands a rededication to one's own vow.

Some other areas in which trained religious women might contribute invaluable service have been scarcely explored. Sister Maria Mercedes, chairman of the sociology department at the College of Notre Dame of Maryland, who was given leave of absence from her academic assignment to serve as director of the division of information and research of the National Conference of Catholic Charities in Washington is an example of this type of work. Opportunities for part-time contributed summer work with local service organizations are being explored by several congregations, work in which even those not specifically trained in social service can contribute. "There is always a need for skilled typists, for file clerks, for some one to answer the telephone, for receptionists," said one mother provincial; "the sisters who take over these jobs free a trained worker for the specific and specialized work he is equipped to do. In addition, the sisters, especially those who work in suburbia, come into contact with poverty and suffering, and achieve an awareness that will be a much more cogent factor in effective teaching than purely theoretical knowledge has been."

Some congregations have been engaged in part-time work in county institutions: hospitals, sanitaria, and homes for the incurable or aged, bringing to the often overworked and understaffed hospital personnel release from pressure, and to the patients an affection which is pathetically welcome. This year for the third year the postulants of my own province spent their Christmas serving trays and helping to feed patients at County General Hospital, Milwaukee, an aid which was not only appreciated by the patients, but by the harassed superintendent who remarked gratefully that it is difficult to get help to work on Christmas.

The gift of self is an essential element of religious poverty, for the vow which does not find expression in giving is no living of the evangelical counsel, even if the room of the individual religious is as stripped of personal possessions as a death cell. In the *Decree on the Apostolate of the Laity*, the Council advises the Catholic layman to seek and find the needy to help them; the religious woman has an equal obligation to become personally involved in helping the poor to help themselves. Encounter with poverty means a realization of how little one needs. Father Martin Carrabine, beloved director of CISCA for many years, used to tell Chicago religious that it would be a salutary thing if in addition to their yearly retreat each of them would annually ride the Madison Avenue bus through Skid Row.

Some of the tensions as well as the dialogue currently being carried on in religious congregations concerning poverty revolve around the necessity for the contemporary nun to be professionally involved in activities which require an outlay of funds a good many citizens simply could not afford, and the parallel necessity in our personal life to maintain detachment. Father Häring, discussing this matter, holds that as a general rule the religious should use courageously all those things which make the apostolate effective and which save manpower, since the most precious property any congregation has are the sisters. But he also warns that, in personal life, wants should be modest.

The problem is basically whether the peculium is consistent with the vow, whether the religious would understand the problems of the poor better were she to buy her own soap and toothpaste, or purchase her noon lunch in the school cafeteria from an allotted budget (although certainly the naïveté of many sisters about economic realities makes some such plan seem educationally practical). Does the religious, both communally and individually, offer witness to the world of Christ's salvific action on behalf of those who, like the *anawim,* depend upon him? The manner of this witness will vary according to the environment, circumstances, and conditions of the sister's apostolate. The musician may need to have her professional background enriched by attendance at a symphony or opera; her companions' personal musical and cultural growth might be met by listening to the same symphony on TV or radio as the vast majority of average citizens are forced to do. The teacher of contemporary drama may need to attend the theater on occasion, but certainly she will go no more frequently than her secular colleague for whom box-office prices are often prohibitive. Conventions, conferences, workshops are not luxuries but obligations for teachers, nurses, social service workers, if they are to be aware of progress in the field. But every religious who has ever attended one of these knows the alternatives such an occasion offers her for choices which witness to her love of poverty.

The question is never, "How much may I have within the framework of my vow?" but "How much can I give to show my love?" As Father Daniel Berrigan points out, "The poor man is man himself. As one veers away from the truth of his poverty, he turns aside from God, from his brother, from himself. He becomes alienated, a man obsessed by illusion. . . . And on the contrary, when one is faithful to the truth of his poverty, the needle's eye bursts apart, the narrow way widens, the truth of existence opens up. One becomes fit for the community, a meeting ground for the hope of man, worthy of experiencing Christ." [10]

It is toward this goal that the vow is aimed; it is with this objective in mind that the religious clears her life of the unnecessary clutter which, even for the detached religious, tends to accumulate periodically. Because she knows that her heart is not limitless in its capacity, that if it is crowded with things there will be little room for Christ and the poor in whom he is most luminously present, her renewal in this regard will, in all probability, result in her having not more but less. She will see that what she has she does not have for herself but that, through her vow of poverty, she may give it to others.

SIX

The Cloistered Contemplative

SISTER TERESA
CARMELITE MONASTERY
PEWAUKEE, WISCONSIN

Since to talk about areas in which the author has only theoretical knowledge seemed to be incompatible with the purposes of this book, I have asked Carmelite Sister Teresa, a former student and warm friend, to describe the contemplative life and its adjustments to the contemporary world.

"Break your alabaster box . . . Give all—and ever." These words of a cloistered contemplative nun sound the keynote for the dialogue and consideration of the relevance of the contemplative nun in the world today.

By taking a long look at this facet of "the treasure hidden in the field, the pearl of great price," the beauty and meaning of the canonical contemplative life will come into clearer focus. According to the definition of Pius XII in his Apostolic Constitution *Sponsa Christi* (Article 2, para. 2):

The heading canonical contemplative life does not refer to that interior and theological life to which all souls living in religion, and even in the world, are called, and which each one may lead within himself anywhere, but to the external profession of religious life which, either through cloistered life, through pious exercises of prayer and mortification, or through the work of cloistered nuns, is so directed toward interior contemplation that the whole of the life and every activity can be easily and effectively penetrated by Him Who is sought.*

The cloistered nun separates herself from the world so that "the whole of her life and every activity can be easily and effectively penetrated by God." Nor is she seeking herself, her own comfort or leisure, but rather the Beloved who has called her.

This call from God is the mystery of vocation. From all eternity the Father knew every individual person in his Son. How vast and varied are his plans for each. It is in following this plan, in man's passionate attachment to the will of God for him, that each person finds "the things that are for his peace." So, too, the contemplative nun has received a specific and personal invitation to seek God, to serve him in a life of prayer and sacrifice, a life separated from the world, but which, if it is lived generously, effectively embraces every person.

We have but to recall St. Matthew's account of the anointing at Bethany to know the mind of Christ in regard to this life devoted primarily to the worship and service of God.

Now when Jesus was in Bethany, in the house of Simon, the leper, a woman came up to him with an alabaster jar of precious ointment, and she poured it on his head as he reclined at table. But when the disciples saw this they were indignant, and said, 'To what purpose is this waste?' 'for this might have been sold for much and given to the poor.'

Bus Jesus, perceiving it, said to them, 'Why do you trouble the woman? She has done me a good turn. For the poor you have always with you, but you do not always have me' (Mt 26:6–11).

Does this mean that God wants all men to hide themselves in a cloister, to forget about helping the poor directly, to

*Whenever "contemplative," "cloistered," or "nun" is used in this chapter it is to be understood in the light of this definition of canonical, contemplative nun.

stop their active work in building the earth? Obviously not. It does mean that God is master of his creatures with the right to set some apart to devote the whole of their lives to the service of his worship, to render to him an unceasing chorus of praise and adoration. It is hoped that speculation on Martha and Mary, contemplative versus active life and which of them is more perfect, has finally come to an end. The contemplative nun is not of a spiritual "elite." She perhaps realizes this better than anyone else. Such classes and distinctions have no place in Christ's Mystical Body where all are brothers with different functions. That the number of vocations to the canonical contemplative life is small is no argument in favor of an elite group. God, like the king in the Gospels, sits down to plan in advance the forces he has and needs to win the battle. Many more men will be needed to fight in the front lines of the world than to hold the fortress from within. God's personal call to each individual, when met with a total response, is undoubtedly the most perfect for that person, whatever concrete form of life it takes. Each person must simply stand before God and, filled with love and gratitude, pronounce his *fiat:* "let it be done to me as you will."

St. Teresa of Avila rejoiced that she was "a daughter of the Church," and every cloistered nun also finds joy in being the daughter of this most wonderful Mother, Holy Church. She, in her turn, continues to approve and encourage the canonical contemplative life among her members. Pius XII in his radio address to cloistered nuns in 1958 said:

> This contemplative life . . . is a road which leads to God Who constitutes its beginning and its end, maintains its impetus and fills all . . . The primacy of meditation and of contemplation of God and divine truth is above all other means of perfection; is above all practices, is above all forms of organizations and federations—this is what we want to emphasize and to recall with all of Our authority.

Contemplation, then, is a *means* to holiness. This cannot be stressed too much. In itself it is not holiness, nor is it the

only way to holiness and union with God. But if we recall
the mystery of vocation, then we see clearly that for those
whom God calls to the contemplative life as recognized by
the Church, it is the usual and most perfect way, the
straight and narrow road ascending to God.

When redistributing the gifts of candles he had received
on February 2, 1961, Pope John XXIII said, "The first
destination to religious houses of more rigid mortification
and penance is intended to affirm once again the pre-emi-
nence of the duties of worship and complete consecration
of life to prayer over any form of apostolate; and at the same
time it emphasizes the greatness and the necessity of vocations for this kind of life." In 1962 in his letter to religious
women the same pontiff wrote: "The Church will always
encourage its daughters who, in order to conform more
perfectly to the call of the Divine Master, give themselves in
the contemplative life."

Prayer and sacrifice are usually linked when speaking of
the apostolate of the contemplative, for true prayer is not
possible without sacrifice, and sacrifice is prayer in action.
Perhaps it would be well to digress from our survey of what
the Church says of cloistered life to consider this point of
sacrifice, mortification, and penance and their meaning in
the world today.

Has any age known the anguish and suffering of our era?
Poverty and destitution, sickness and war throw their
shadows over our lives. What then shall we say of penance
and sacrifice lovingly embraced? Foolishness? A stumbling
block? No, rather it is the love of Christ which impels the
nun, the ardent and effective desire to share in his im-
molation that she may also share in his redemptive work,
the salvation of every person. Trials and sacrifices are simply
the means by which God invites all to a more perfect self-
giving in love. Pain, if it is not transcended and united to
the sufferings and cross of Christ, is meaningless and unbear-
able. Therefore, if we love our fellow men we must greatly
desire and take measures to alleviate their misery, and this
with all the material aids and personal resources at our

disposal. We must, however, offer them spiritual strength also, by showing them the possibility of becoming one with Christ and his redemptive suffering. Sister M. Cuthbert, CSMM, wrote, "The cross of Christ does not announce to the world that suffering exists, but that a path has been found through it that leads to salvation." The cloistered nun, sharing in the cross of Christ, also shares in its announcement to the world and leads a multitude along that path to salvation.

According to St. Thomas, "Everything which is offered to God, so that man's spirit may be uplifted to him, may be called a sacrifice." Suffering, as considered above, comes from God, through circustances, persons, and events. Asceticism, which includes penance, mortification, and self-denial, must be initiated by man himself. Asceticism can be divided into will training and self-discipline, which are necessary for every person to grow to personal, spiritual maturity; and mortification and penance which should flow from the abundance of one's love, from the need to express bodily, exteriorly, the interior disposition of self-giving to God.

These distinctions are the basis for the Church's changes in her laws of fasting. And cloistered communities are keeping pace with the Church. Definite changes have been made not only in regard to food, but also to rest and clothing. The Lenten black fast, which allowed no eggs or dairy products, is no longer kept. Most communities observe a fast from September 14 until Easter, in which one main meal is taken at noon with an adequate breakfast and evening collation. Nourishing, balanced, well-prepared food puts the emphasis on ordinariness rather than minimum quantity, on personal mortification as opposed to delicacy of taste. Nor does this exclude specials and treats on feast days. Many nuns take a cup of coffee in the morning before mental prayer and the Sacrifice of the Mass. Far from introducing relaxations, these changes have made the nun physically and mentally more alert, more capable of full participation in her intense life of prayer.

Likewise, a good night's rest is normally essential. It is reasonable to forego some sleep at times to spend time in prayer to God or service to one's neighbor, but not simply to endure discomfort. Charity usually becomes difficult to exercise when one is tired and irritable from lack of sleep. Communities are experimenting with daily schedules to insure this necessary rest. Straw mattresses are being replaced by inexpensive cotton ones, not because one could not sleep well on straw, but rather for the practical purposes of cleanliness and the inability, in many cases, to obtain straw.

Lightweight, washable materials are now used in making habits. Wool, which once was the cloth of the poor, has become far too expensive for religious seeking to identify with the poor. Central heating in monasteries has made warm, heavy habits unnecessary in winter. That hot, itchy wool may once have been considered a penance cannot be denied. Now, however, the nun is more likely to find her penance in fatigue from productive labor, to cite but one far more salutary and reasonable example. As Pius XII has so beautifully stated in his encyclical *Mystici Corporis:* "Deep mystery, this, subject of inexhaustible meditation: that the salvation of many depends on the prayers and voluntary penances which the members of the Mystical Body of Jesus Christ offer for that intention."

Pope Paul VI has taken opportunities to reiterate the statements of his predecessors affirming the tremendous force which the contemplative life is in the Church. In a letter to the superior general of the Discalced Carmelites dated May 3, 1965, he wrote:

Holy Church demands from your Religious that they bear witness to those genuine values which will never fade, to the benefit of modern man, who is too much given to earthly desires and too engrossed in worldly pursuits and cares. They will achieve this by their unremitting dedication to prayer, which, if God so pleases, will lead them to the summit of contemplation; by their self-abnegation; by the example of their ready obedience, by preserving the candor of chastity."

It is these values of which our Holy Father speaks which will form the basis of dialogue in the rest of this chapter.

But first a final word on cloistered life, this time from the *Decree on the Appropriate Renewal of the Religious Life* (#7).

Members of the communities which are totally dedicated to contemplation give themselves to God alone in solitude and silence, and through constant prayer and ready penance. No matter how urgent may be the needs of the active apostolate, such communities will always have a distinguished part to play in Christ's Mystical Body, where all members have not the same function (Rom. 12:4). For they offer God a choice sacrifice of praise. They brighten God's people with the richest splendors of sanctity. By their example they motivate this people; by imparting a hidden, apostolic fruitfulness, they make this people grow. Thus they are the glory of the Church and an overflowing fountain of heavenly graces.

Every nun rejoices in these words of approval and encouragement from the Council fathers. They contain a challenge and urgent invitation for her to speak to the men of her times, to let her life permeate the whole world in her witness to Christ. She too must seek him where he is, and bring him where he wishes to be, into the lives of all men. Thus all will truly be formed into the family of God.

How does the cloistered nun speak to the world and what does she say? Before all else she declares that God *is*. He is not dead, for as the great Apostle says, "In him we live and move and have our being." He is the life of our life. This life of the nun, therefore, is utterly meaningless if God does not exist. Priests and other religious engaging in active works of the apostolate have something tangible to show for their hours of labor and dedicated service to mankind. Even were there no God, their work would have humanitarian and social value. Now it is a known fact that human beings must have goals to work toward, a purpose for living, or they become listless, joyless, "faceless" people who find life intolerable. But joy is too evident to be missed as it shines from the face of a nun. She is a woman who is so sure of the God whom she loves and serves, to whom she has consecrated her whole life, that she radiates a quiet peace and happiness. She has found the profound fulfillment of her whole being, for man's being is one long craving for God, and she encounters him in every moment of her life. Her hours spent in prayer are but the prolongation of her continual presence to the Lord and her interior converse with him. By her life of worship given to God she speaks of his transcendence as also of his total supremacy over his creatures and their primary duty to him before all else. By the fullness of love which her heart bears to him she tells of God's immanence, of his Spirit dwelling in the heart of every man. Christ lives in her and in her brothers. Thus her presence in the world is a sign of Christ's presence. Her belief in him brings to birth and nourishes faith in the hearts of all men. It is not what she does but what she is that speaks so clearly to the world. Because of this life of faith in God, truly lived and spread among men, she confidently knows that when the Son of Man returns he will find faith upon the earth.

John the Baptist announced the imminent approach of the kingdom of God. The contemplative, in her prophetic role in the Church, witnesses to the reality of that same kingdom already present within us and around us. She echoes the words of Jesus, "Fear not, little flock, for the Father has determined to give you his kingdom." In the light of this truth the nun bends all her efforts toward establishing the reign of Christ in her own heart and in every man's. Poverty, willingly embraced, speaks of riches which are not of this world, for where "your heart is, there is your treasure also." As she empties her heart of desires for many things, room is made for the kingdom of God to enter.

The cloistered nun, at least in America, does not live in destitution. Work is a healthful and necessary part of her day. By the labor of mind and hands contemplative communities are striving toward greater self-support and maintenance. This makes their witness to poverty a more genuine sign to men as they share in a positive way the same fatigue and concerns of the poor. Designing and sewing vestments, printing, writing, gardening, and the making of hosts for the Sacrifice of the Mass are some of their productive labors. It is not the use of necessary things or the development of all the resources of the earth that hinders the coming of the kingdom, for, in truth, man in his work is helping to build a new heaven and a new earth. His activity in the world is good. It is only in the excessive desire and attachment to things that man's mind is clouded, his reason dulled, and his freedom hampered. The poverty of the nun is a sign to men, pointing the way to true freedom and openness to Christ's reign in poor and empty hearts.

The vow of chastity taken for the sake of the kingdom of God could be termed a vow of love. It is total commitment and surrender of her entire person to Christ. By her vow the nun gives her love to God and receives it back from his hands, transformed. The love of Christ is in truth poured forth into her heart, giving new and greater capacities for love of her brothers throughout the world. Perhaps this is a point most difficult to understand. Experiencing this deep universal love growing within oneself is the only conclusive proof. But an explanation of this seeming paradox is possible. To speak of detachment is to call to mind images of cold and distant faces, the antithesis of the warm love and respect for every person which is at the heart of the Gospel message. But these uninviting pictures are far from the reality. True detachment is the other side of the coin of perfect attachment to the will of God in which one is able to will peacefully all that he wills. "Since there is nothing imperfect in our Supreme Good, everything he gives us must be for our good" (St. Teresa). The detached heart is free from excessive emotion that might blind the intellect in seeing what is really for the good and weaken and prevent the will from choosing this good. Chastity makes possible and effective this clear vision and ardent desire for that which is really best for each person.

Contemplatives make their own the prayer of St. Thérèse of Lisieux, "That I, through my life of union with you, may be mother to many souls." Chastity tells the world of the primacy of spiritual motherhood because of the nearness of the kingdom of God. Praying "Our Father," the nun stands before God in union with all men, bringing their needs, their love, to him who is the Father of all. Free to pray for every man, the prayer of the nun is catholic and all-embracing in spirit and interests.

In our rapidly changing, technological world, silence is almost unknown. To a great extent, man has forgotten how to be silent. Not knowing or experiencing the beauty and worth of silence, he does not try to create it, for silence is creative and must be created. It is a positive value and not merely the absence of noise. This is the silent message the cloistered nun delivers to the world. "The Father uttered one Word, his Word, his Son; he utters it eternally in an eternal silence. It is in silence that the soul hears" (St. John of the Cross). Contemplative nuns all live a life of silence. Although the external forms and rules of each order vary as to the amount of speaking permitted, the idea and purpose behind the externals is always the same: to be silent interiorly that she may be attentive to the Spirit abiding within her. As the blind man has a more acute sense of touch, so the silent man can listen and perceive with greater awareness. God does not usually speak with words, but communicates with men through every circumstance, every contact with another person, every moment of their lives. Moments of silence help to integrate one's actions, experiences, and knowledge. Man is able to see himself more clearly, to have deeper empathy in his relations with others. Silence that is not a void but is filled with awareness of God's presence is healing to troubled minds. Far more than mood music, silence has the power to calm the soul, restoring peace to the whole man. The contemplative life preserves this ideal of silence and shows it to men. By the peace in her own life the nun invites others to set aside minutes of living silence in each day. The monastery is an oasis of stillness where men may come for brief spaces of time to relearn this most valuable art, to rediscover the Spirit living within them.

Prayer is born and grows in silence. It is friendship with God in which man converses with him and shares his most intimate self, for he knows the hearts of men. In this most perfect and satisfying I-thou relationship man comes to experience a love that does not grow weary or impatient, but rather has the effective power of calling forth a true response of love. In prayer God speaks his creative words to men. He offers them a share in his life by grace. It is through this grace that man is made capable of receiving the Father's Word, his Son.

The Liturgy: the Holy Sacrifice of the Mass and the *Opus Dei,* the Divine Office, form, so to speak, the hub of the wheel around which all the activities of the cloistered nun revolve. We are speaking now of the structure of the life, for God is the inmost center toward which everything, including the rites of the Liturgy, converge. The Community Mass unites all as the whole Mystical Body of Christ participates in the Sacrifice and Sacrament. Like the unchanging canon of the Mass, the nun's silent life is the unchanging prayer and sacrifice that prepares the world for its consecration, its oneness with the mystery of all things which are Christ's. She goes forth from Mass to continue living it throughout the day, to show forth Christ who dwells now more fully in her. The Divine Office, recited in English, which all nuns are authorized by the Church to say, joins her to the official prayer of the Church offering continual praise to God. The hours of the Office wisely divide the day so that the nun is always returning to the great work of her life which is prayer. She believes that many things can be accomplished "only by prayer and fasting." As an active member of the praying Church she goes to her "post" as surely as the men fighting in the trouble spots of the world. She is a vital force in missionary work, in scientific research, social work, civil rights movements, and the war on poverty —wherever men are seeking to do the Father's will, for she prays with the psalmist that God may "prosper the work of our hands for us."

We speak of faith in the power of prayer, but it would be far truer to speak of faith and confidence in the power of God to whom we pray. This faith in God is essential for the cloistered religious, forming as it does the foundation upon which her apostolate is built. She places her trust in the promise of Christ, "Whatever you ask in prayer, if you believe, it shall be given to you." "Ask and you shall receive." We know from the Gospels that this was the only requirement Jesus asked of those who came to him in need. "Do you believe I can do this? If you have faith it shall be done to you. Your faith has made you whole." Prayer is a powerful instrument in the hands of those who trust not in their own strength, but in the infinite strength of God. While recognizing the necessity of activity and the responsibility of each person to develop talents in the service of the Lord, the nun is a quiet reminder to all that men will always be tools in the hands of God. Their work will succeed as long as it is his work. It will fail when they cease to look to him for guidance and help in fulfilling his will. In the face of apparent failure the contemplative prays:

Where my feet will not take me;
there I will kneel down.
Where my hands fail me;
there I will fold them.—Gertrude von Le Fort

Peace has been mentioned many times in this brief look at cloistered life, and what it hopes to share in dialogue with the modern world. Peace is desired by all and possessed by few. We hear of wars and rumors of war, of the breakdown of family life, or riots and unrest. Still the straining toward peace is inborn in every person. There is no magic formula for acquiring this good. The late John F. Kennedy said often he would have only the peace of a good conscience to support him. No man individually can stop wars and hatred. But each can and must work to establish peace in his own soul. Cloistered religious beg God to aid them to bring about this ordering of their own interior life and then to let it spread outward, creating union and harmony among men. It is a tremendous task which challenges man. Shall he throw up his hands in despair? Rather let all turn to the Gospel message, living its principles in their own lives, influencing the people who form their circle of encounter.

The contemplative realizes that man's action is always limited. Undaunted by this thought she endeavors to become the leaven which Jesus speaks of that eventually will lighten the whole mass. She calls to all men to follow her lead in their quest for peace. If this seems idealistic, impractical, and wholly irrelevant in our times, let us recall and believe what Christ has told us: "With men this is impossible, but with God all things are possible."

"Your life is hidden with Christ in God." This hidden life of the nun appears to be opposed to the values of the modern mind. Great emphasis is being placed on the importance of fulfilling one's personality which, so it would seem, cannot be done unless a person asserts himself and satisfies all the longings and desires which arise within him. When women are championing their rights and equality in society and the Church, when Catholic action and missionary work of all kinds are coming to the fore, and witness is so necessary in the life of the Church, an enclosed life may tend to become incomprehensible to many people. That each person must reach fulfillment in order to attain holiness and wholeness is true, but at times our concept of true fulfillment and the means to it can be faulty. A woman with an authentic contemplative vocation must be a most balanced, wholesome person, able to integrate every part of her life into that whole which constitutes her being. She has common sense, joy, perspective in looking at life, good understanding, and varying talents. More than likely, had she not received this wonderful call from God to belong to him alone, she would have been a wife and mother. She is all woman. Totally dedicated and surrendered to the will of God, she chooses this hidden life in order to be completely available to him, to be constantly in his service in the work of the salvation of the world. It is through this free self-giving to God and her fellow men in prayer and sacrifice that she finds perfect fulfillment.

Not only do nuns leave their enclosure for absolutely necessary hospitalization, but also for annual physicals, eye and dental care. Workshops, intermonastery meetings, and educational courses in various fields, especially theology, psychology, music, and art, are attended by nuns. At times, professional people are given permission to enter the enclosure to give instruction in these areas of education as well as in manual skills. Formation programs for the young women entering a contemplative community are being adapted and renewed to meet the educational and psychological needs of the times. Previously each monastery trained its own candidates. Now common novitiates and juniorates are being considered to provide competent formation in the various aspects of human, Christian, and religious development.

The enclosure is a sign and expression of withdrawal from the world for one reason only: that the nun may devote her whole person to the worship and service of God. Formerly enclosure meant that the religious should not see people outside the enclosure or be seen by them. Most nuns today feel this prohibition is no longer valid or helpful. Thus black grate veils worn over the face when visiting or when workmen enter the enclosure are neither a sign to men nor a safeguard for mature women and are no longer in use. Chain-link fences and similar enclosure walls are beginning to replace the solid brick or wooden wall, at much lower cost, in keeping with poverty. To retain some kind of fence in the outside enclosure and some kind of material separation such as a single grate in the visiting rooms within the monastery is to retain the sign of withdrawal from the world and to provide a necessary safeguard for silence and solitude, essentials in the contemplative life. Enclosure is not meant to be a penance or means of antisocial withdrawal from people. For the woman who is called and freely embraces this life, it is simply the most effective means of accomplishing her apostolate, which is constant prayer.

A consideration of freedom and obedience has been placed last so that what has preceded might prepare the way for a clearer understanding of the profound and longed-for existential fact of freedom and its collaborator and necessary companion, obedience. The vow and virtue of obedience have for their essential end the acceptance of the will of God as manifested in one's life and an adequate response to it. Thus it is the surest way of knowing how to "do the truth in charity." Modern man places independence very high on his scale of values. Thinking obedience is opposed to this, he often finds it unworthy of practice. But what makes men truly free and independent? First, a humble recognition and acceptance of their total dependence on God, for they are his creatures, created new each moment and sustained only through the power and love of the Father. To accept this fact is to accept the truth which will make men free. The second element of freedom is detachment from self, other creatures, and material things, detachment as has been discussed above. When a person is influenced and forced by external circumstances—his culture, society, the *status quo*, advertisement, pressure groups, and human respect—his life is shaped and directed for him by these very forces. He becomes their slave, not planning and forming his own destiny. On the other hand, the more a person is detached from creatures and circumstances, the easier it is for him to stand apart from the situation and evaluate it objectively. He is free. He is capable of making choices in depth, directing his own life and creating his life situations. The will of God becomes his only concern, the passionate desire of his heart. Gradually the free man can say in truth, "I do always the things that please the Father." This is radical freedom far from the license and irresponsibility which too often parade as "liberal" and free.

It has almost become a cliché to say that authority is service. Every real superior, however, holds this truth and finds in it support, strength, and courage. Her desire to be identified with Christ is given new opportunities for realization in fulfilling the duties of her office, for he said, "Behold, I stand in the midst of you as one who serves." True, deep respect for the human person is a value which man rightly holds in high regard. Nor can respect be demanded; it can only be freely given. Obedience is given to lawful authority, respect is due to all. Thus the obedience given to a superior who stands in the place of God is obedience given to God. It is to know and do his will. It is the authority every religious freely chooses to obey for the rest of her life. If the nun truly loves and respects each of her sisters in Christ this will certainly include her superiors.

However, many of the formalities of respect observed by religious in the past no longer bring with them the force of truth. Those that have become empty signs are being changed—for example, kneeling whenever one speaks to the superior, kissing her hand in certain ceremonies, and bowing the head toward her as a sign of recognition. These and similar changes encourage personal responsibility for developing such essential virtues as loyalty, courtesy and kindness, and a deep appreciation of the dignity of each person.

Modern man speaks of essentials, essences, and the abandonment of all that is excessive and false. But this is not something new; rather it is the eschatogolical sign of hope which we find in the Gospels as poverty of spirit. The contemplative is constantly striving to attain and witness to this value. By detachment and the stripping of all that is not God for the sake of God, the nun seeks to empty herself and be emptied. Thus she stands before God in naked faith, in pure hope, having nothing to offer him but her very being which is slowly transformed by love into love. This doctrine may seem hard and radical. It is both. But the generosity of man today, his search for freedom and truth, if he will but realize it, is a search for this radical self-giving to God. He will be secure in God's hands if he will only cast himself into them without reserve. This is pre-eminently the most relevant message the contemplative nun gives to the world. It is filled with challenge and the firm expectation of the fulfillment of all Christ's promises in her and in every man who hears and believes.

In conclusion we turn our gaze once more to the Gospels, the source from which our life must flow. In St. John's sixth chapter is related Our Lord's discourse on the bread of life. He spoke of the Word and faith by which men are nourished. Then, using the same symbol of bread, he told them that he is the true bread which has come down from heaven. Then follows the revelation containing both command and promise. It was so shocking and incomprehensible to the natural man that many could not accept it. "He who eats my flesh and drinks my blood has life everlasting and I will raise him up on the last day." Many said, "This is a hard saying. Who can listen to it?" And they turned away and followed him no longer. But what did Jesus do? Did he call them back and retract what he had said? Did he water down his teaching and make it easy for them? He could have done this and increased his following. But it would not have been the truth. He let them leave him.

Something similar takes place in the dialogue between the cloistered contemplative nun and the modern world. Her life of faith with all that it requires of sacrifice and courage, of strong love and ardent clinging to the will of God, often without tangible results, is a hard saying in our age of action and comfort, where visible results are the criterion of success. Still it is a leaven that cannot be kept from spreading, a light that will continue to shine and give light to all men who open themselves to it. For there are always people who will not turn away, but will let every good influence in their lives shape and mold them into Christ. If she tries to convince others, it is only that, believing in the values this life holds out to them, their own lives may be deepened as they draw closer to the Father through Christ in his Holy Spirit. Whether men accept this witness or not, her silent, constant prayer rising to God establishes a living contact between man and his Creator. Even though they are not aware of it, because of Christ and his praying Church, untold numbers of individuals share in the grace-life which is God, living and giving himself in love. Her presence in the world must make Christ present and be a force which will gradually help to bring into reality the prayer of Jesus, "That all may be one, even as you, Father, in me and I in you. That they also may be one in us." (Jn 17:21)

Through her life of prayer and consecration, the contemplative nun is an intimate collaborator with God to fill the hungry soul with his life, to heal the broken heart with his mercy and love, giving peace to troubled minds and Wisdom, who is God himself, to all men searching for knowledge and truth. God is Spirit and can only be communicated, loved, and worshiped in spirit and truth. This the nun lives and proclaims to all the world today.

The world speaks to the nun of the wonders of creation,

the power and knowledge God has given to man to transform the earth. It tells of man's genuine quest for the real, the good, and the beautiful, of his desire to receive love and give himself in a return of love. May the world also say to her: We believe in you.

In your life we see a promise of peace and joy for all men.

In your faith and confidence we find new courage.

In your obedience we learn how to be free.

In your prayer we are strengthened.

In your love we find warmth and security.

In you we find Christ and so recognize him in ourselves and our brothers.

SEVEN

Chastity Is Love

It is an interesting fact that while the celibacy of the priest has been debated informally and formally, in small clerical gatherings and during the formal sessions of Vatican II, as well as on the front pages of secular and diocesan newspapers, the relevance of the vow of chastity for nuns has not been questioned with anything like the same emotional heat. The reasons for this paradox are not simple, nor do the superficial explanations sometimes offered seem adequate to explain the contrast: the greater enclosure of religious women, their involvement in more femininely oriented works, which provide sublimated satisfaction for the normal sexual drive.

This is not to say that virginity presents no natural problems to women, or that sisters who leave religious life after obtaining a dispensation do not ever marry. Certainly some of them do, but they do not appear to have marriage as motivation for leaving the convent as frequently as priests, if the reasons quoted by the press concerning the latter are to be believed.

Perhaps this is the place briefly to face up to the whole touchy problem of defections, a problem which has received considerable publicity in the past few years, and about which a good many undocumented statements have been made. One hears and reads of increasing numbers of religious who have left their congregations in articles illustrated by

a half dozen to a dozen examples of the more newsworthy
and more dramatic. I have been asked innumerable times
by interested laymen whether I think the trend in this
direction is greater in the last decade or not. My inter-
rogators have always been a bit surprised when I answered
frankly that I am in no position to know, and I seriously
doubt whether many people are. After all, they argue, I am
a nun; I ought to know what is going on.

But religious congregations are autonomous, and a statement made by one or about one would not necessarily apply
to others. Statistical variations exist from congregation to
congregation, and provinces differ from provinces even
within the same community. Therefore, any data I might
have concerning my own province could not be interpreted
as accurate for the other eight North American provinces of
the School Sisters of Notre Dame. Numbers isolated from
other pertinent data are unreliable. An illustration from
the opposite end of the vocation scale, for which I do have
some numbers, may demonstrate this: it would be false to
deduce that the newly formed SSND De Kalb province is
alarmingly low in new vocations by comparing its eight
novices with the Mequon province, which has forty-one,
unless one were to take into account the fact that the new
province has a total of 332 professed sisters as contrasted
with the mother province's 1725. Similarly, any adding up
of losses for a particular congregation or province must take
the total number of sisters into account in addition to other
factors.

When I was discussing this matter two years ago with Dan
Herr, president of Thomas More Association, he asked me
to hazard a guess as to the number of sisters of our province
who had left the congregation in the past year after having
taken perpetual vows. When I later checked my presumption
that there might have been five, I discovered that I had three
too many; the total number had been two.

But even four-figure numbers need to be weighed in a
total context before generalizations are made. Some one
noted recently that 5000 fewer sisters were listed in the
National Catholic Directory than in the previous year. It is

a startling number if one does not remember that this does
not necessarily mean that 5000 women left religious life.
Death takes its annual toll, a tighter screening of applicants
and later vocational decisions account for at least part of the
smaller number of postulants. But even if the 5000 did
represent sisters who had asked for and received dispensation
from their vows, it would be a slim 3 per cent of the total
170,000 American nuns. Three per cent seems scarcely de-
serving of either panic or publicity, and yet religious have
been on the receiving end of both.

I have no intention of attempting to probe the reasons
why religious leave the convent other than to underline
what I stated earlier, that the vow of chasity is not in an
appreciable number of cases the deciding factor.

This vow remains today, as in the past, a significant sign
of the sister's total dedication of self. As with poverty and
obedience, the nun does not make a renunciation of something she considers evil or dangerous, but gives to God the
gift which, in the natural order, is his greatest gift to her—
her body with its full potentiality of procreation and the
marital love in which it would flower. Because she appreciates marriage she renounces it. She does not reject love, but
opens her heart to all those whose lives will cross hers. A
Hindu friend commenting on religious virginity unknow-
ingly gave a contemporary paraphrase of St. Paul (I Cor
7:34–35) when he said, "You give up the love of one man
so that you can the more easily love many." This self-giving
is, of course, rooted in love for God; it is not a negative act,
a sacrifice, but an affirmation as positive as that by which
the bride binds herself to her husband. We do not vow
chastity to something but to Someone.

Contemporary theology rejects the earlier terminology by
which the sister was called the bride of Christ (the cere-
monial for the taking of vows parallels that of the marriage
ceremony), terming her instead the witness and sign of that
unity which the Church, the whole of mankind, is called to
form with God in Christ. Consecrated virginity is a deeper
manifestation of the witness every Christian bears through
baptism of sonship and brotherhood.

Father Schleck has pointed out that while the sister is a sign of many things—of the fact that God exists, that he can touch the soul in a most intimate way, that he can ask a soul to live for him alone—still she is above all a sign of a greater mystery: that he is love. She reflects the concern of God for souls in a maternal way.[1] While the nun does not become so in order to do an apostolic work, but to dedicate herself completely in virginity to God in love, love is essentially fruitful in action. As someone has shrewdly commented, "Love is good, but love with noodles is better," and the sister discovers early that as her love for God deepens, her love for the people of God expands.

While the virtue of chastity is part of the cardinal virtue of temperance that moderates the use of sexual pleasure, to overemphasize the negative aspects of the vow is to create by implication an unreal, inhuman state of life. It cannot be denied that there was a tendency in the past to emphasize the negative aspects of the virtue, an emphasis that was more the dry flowering of Jansenism and Puritanism than an accurate interpretation of the mind of Christ, who identified his commandment as one of love. Father Andrew Greeley, in discussing the training of an earlier generation when postulants were warned that emotional attachments could get them into trouble, and the goal of true spirituality was to remain emotionally uninvolved with people with whom they worked, notes that there is danger in any human friendship as there is danger in human life.[2] But it is just this involvement in love that justifies the taking of the vow. The form of the involvement will change with the years; the young religious, because she is young, may find the winsomeness of the children she teaches her greatest opportunity, as a woman, and her greatest suffering for the same reason. Childless herself, her woman's heart will find satisfaction in the loving care of other women's children, but it would be dishonest not to recognize the fact that complete natural satisfaction is not achieved. As we have noted, there is a danger here, but there is danger in any human relationship. Simply because there is danger does not mean that we must stop living, or that we stop loving. . . . "We must need people, and yet we

must not need them. We must love them, and yet we must
not be totally dependent upon them. We must be attached
to them, and yet our personality has to be strong enough to
survive in their absence." [3] The consecrated virgin makes
her own the prayer T. S. Eliot places on the lips of Thomas
à Becket, "Teach us to care and not to care."

There is nothing surprising about this tension of opposite
attractions. Scripture refers continually to the *paying* of the
vows, and for all except the novice who dies on her profession morning, it will be a lifelong payment. The French
have a statement which is only half true: *C'est le premier
pas qui coute,* "It is the first step which costs." What the
quotation omits is the correlative fact that it is the first step
which pledges that others will be taken. One has only to see
the rapt expression on the face of the ninety-year-old great-
grandmother, as she holds her fourth generation grandchild
in her arms, to realize that a woman's response to a child has
nothing to do with her age. The nun will feel this natural
deprivation all her life, but her emotional life does find its
balance in service of those whom the providence of God
gives to her love. Consecrated virginity is not spiritually
sterile: rather it is essentially creative. The nun may renounce the expression of sex on the natural plane, but she
does not renounce her womanhood. As the *Dogmatic Constitution on the Church* points out, by virginity, or celibacy,
religious can more easily devote their entire selves to God
alone with an undivided heart. This total continence embraced on behalf of the kingdom of heaven has always been
held in particular honor by the Church as being a sign of
charity and a stimulus toward it, as well as a unique fountain
of spiritual fertility in the world.

The religious woman's vow of chastity is born of a deep
personal love for Christ, a love which grows and expands
with her love for those within whose orbit her own life
moves. Scripture points out the impossibility of loving God,
whom we do not see, if we do not love our neighbor, whom
we do; God is loved with the same heart and, as Father
Boylan points out, in exactly the same degree as we love our
brothers. The sister who does not see her virginal dedication

in this light will become a prey to loneliness and depression if she does not suffer from the even more contracting compensation of selfishness.

Whatever misinterpretations an earlier generation put upon the sister's duty to love, today's young woman is encouraged to be herself in a warmly human although prudent fashion. Purity for her is not a matter of ice, but of fire; the full development of her personality as a woman demands that she be involved in the lives of those she serves. The day is gone, if it ever existed, when the nun separated herself emotionally from her apostolic work.

While St. Ignatius' principle of holy indifference has admittedly produced some inhumanly conceived annotations, the holiest Jesuits of any age have resembled their founder in their uncanny aptitude for friendship. Sisters who make the Spiritual Exercises have demonstrated a similar ability to interpret detachment in its Christian context, and to disassociate it from a cold, mechanical relationship with living human beings. Teilhard de Chardin points out that "Purity in spite of outward appearances is essentially an active virtue, because it concentrates God in us and on those who are subject to our influence . . ." [4] Developing the idea still further, he talks about the great wrong done by those who are insufficiently human, "whose religion, I mean, does not, as its first effect, make them more faithful to the duties and problems of their own day." [5]

The idea that a wholehearted service of God is dehumanizing has no justification. Father Van Zeller points out that Christ came to redeem and sanctify humanity, not to overlay it and restrict its development with the demand of religion.[6] The dedicated religious is entitled to human completeness, and it would be no tribute to God were she other than a wholly balanced individual, a mature woman with all of a mature woman's capacity for friendship and affection.

A recent article in *Commonweal* commented on the concept of spiritual motherhood as a sick self-image.[7] History, however, gives vibrant evidence that spiritual maternity does exist. All of us have heard and read of women, if we have not actually known them, for whom maternity was a biological accident, who have left their infants at the first opportunity in the back pew of a church, in the women's room of a bus station, or on the front porch of a convent. It was spiritual motherhood in the person of the sister which stepped in to take over the nurturing and education of these abandoned children when physical motherhood failed. One may agree that *Cradle Song* is a sentimental and psychologically loaded bit of theater, without feeling obliged to repudiate the role of the religious woman who gives love to unloved children. The religious not only cannot divest herself of her feminine characteristics, she would betray both her vocation and God were she to attempt to do so. Pope Pius XII, commenting on the fact that as a woman she has been endowed by God with maternal instincts which she dare not attempt to destroy, says:

"Every woman is destined to be a mother; a mother in the physical sense of the word, or in a more spiritual and higher but no less real meaning. The Creator has disposed to this end the entire being of woman, her organism, and even more, her spirit, and above all, her exquisite sensibility. So that a woman cannot see and fully understand all the problems of human life otherwise than under a family aspect." [8]

Obviously the nun will not enjoy the deeply satisfying family experience of physical motherhood, or the sustaining affection of a husband, but to equate this lack and its consequent human loneliness with inevitable frustration is to suggest that the God who created a woman's heart is incapable of filling it. Much has been written about personal fulfillment, but there is sufficient evidence that the completely selfless person is also well-rounded; that the incomplete and immature personality is rarely generous and other-centered.

Sister Elaine Marie Prevallet [9] notes that married couples give evidence of the singular, individual character of Christ's redemptive love, while the virgin witnesses to the absolute universality of Christ's love. "Hence marriage and virginity present complementary signs of the nature of Christ's love for the Church: it is a love that touches each individual

individually, and a love that extends to all without exception." [10]

As time and space are narrowed in an electronically controlled world, the sister finds her work expanding, the
opportunities for her to radiate the love of Christ multiplied.
Without relinquishing the standard works of mercy to which
they are committed, congregations have made it possible for
individual members to follow the urging of their hearts in
unusual and specialized areas. Sister Mary Anita, RSM, of St.
Mary's Hospital, San Francisco, for example, teaches medical-
surgical nursing to San Quentin inmates, several of whom
have asked to remain past parole time to complete her one-
year course. "Most of them are just boys," says Sister. "They
want a chance to prove they can be better." Sister Mary
Madonna, SSJ, Minneapolis, shuns sign language in teaching
deaf children; instead she speaks slowly and enunciates
carefully because "The deaf are trapped in their own world
if they use sign language, but if they speak, they are an
integral part of society," she explains. Sister José and the
staff of Marymount College, Boca Raton, Florida, have
completed two summers of service to fifteen hundred migrant
adults and their families, making the complete facilities of
the college available for these summer pilgrims who were
not wanted in the "Gold Coast" towns in Florida's vacation-
land. The National Catholic Conference for Interracial
Justice Traveling Workshop nuns lectured for human rights
in the summer of 1966 in fifty-five institutes in thirty-one
states, traveling 50,000 miles and meeting well over 14,000
participants,—and this during their "vacation." But the list
of possible examples gets longer and longer, as congregation
after congregation grasps the opportunities within its reach,
and sister after sister for whom there is no padlock on the
heart recognizes the human face of poverty. "For them,
charity has become more than mere money and help and
prayer. It has become the love and the understanding that
is meant by charity in the fullness of the term." [11]

And who shall assess the flowering of chastity in the day-
by-day multiplication of selfless acts done in the less dramatic
ordinary occupations which are a part of the professional

life of the teacher, nurse, social worker, the cook, laundress, telephone operator, portress, the baker, and the holy beggars who wear the habit of the Little Sisters of the Poor? A cynical world has long considered it a miracle that three dozen women, or three, could live together for a lifetime, but it has not seen the relationship between this fact, between the affection and friendship which ripens through the years between members of the same community, and the self-giving of the vow of chastity.

As *Perfectae Caritatis* points out,[12] the chastity proper to the religious life is not meant to constrict the heart. "It liberates the human heart in a unique way and causes it to burn with greater love for God and for all mankind."

That dignity and reserve will continue to be safeguards of the sister's chastity is no cause for surprise when one considers the prudence demanded of a married woman in her relationship with others. In fact, the same type of healthy interest, intelligent and unaffected concern in the professional and social areas of her life mark the nun, in whom the vow of chastity is really operative.

Sister Mary Bettina, SSND, in a story for the Newman Center paper at Northern State University, De Kalb, Illinois, summarized what virginity means to the religious. Said Sister Bettina:

Virginity is something one doesn't usually talk about. He lives it, and forgets it, because it has become for him something like the air—an invisible element in which he moves and which he therefore takes for granted.

I compare dedicated chastity to the air—or to the water which frees at the same time that it supports the swimmer—because it is more than a physical abstinence. It is a way of thinking. Speaking as an amateur psychologist, I can see a different approach to life in people who have dedicated their chastity to God. Granted, virginity is their gift, and one doesn't give gifts for a reason. But the giving does make of a person something he could not be if he did not give.

Being an element which both frees and sustains, chastity can easily be forgotten about. And in fact, a chastity conscious of itself is a contradiction, an anomaly as impossible as selfish love. Yet other people are always aware of one's virginity, with the marveling respect which those not dedicated to it invariably have. And when they call our attention to it as if it were a natural element, suddenly are tempted to look deep into the waters on which we walk and, like St. Peter, to think that we're probably going to have to sink.

Only when we are unaware of our sacrifice, in other words, can we make it. A virginity self-consciously given leads to the martyr-complex and makes one calculate the benefits to be derived from his sacrifice. No one—regardless of for whom or what he is sacrificing—can afford to think that way.

Scripture, on the other hand, gives a natural, cheerful picture of unself-conscious virginity. We who have given up our ability to have children are described in symbolic terms as following Christ wherever he goes and singing a song no one else is able to learn.

I refuse to look on this proud, close, singing companionship as a reward for martyrdom. To me it is an ordinary day-to-day state of mind, and I experience this glorious camaraderie right now, not only with Christ but with his people.

This invisible element in which I live, this state of mind which follows from my state of body, opens up to me human relationships undreamt of by others. I have an exclusive man-woman relationship with no one, it is true. But I am engaged in intense personal relationships with all types of people as well as with God.

To a man, I can be a disinterested, unpredatory feminine friend. To a woman I can be a sister, not a rival. To children I am sort of a universal mother, and they are given the instinct to know that they are important to me. I am as proud of all these relationships as I am of the one I have with Christ.

Now I ask you, can anybody call this martyrdom? It is, as Scripture says, not death but life—or rather, an element in which life is carried on. Open as the air, supporting like the water, chastity frees me for God and for all people as long as I forget myself.

EIGHT

The Sister
In Formation

Over the centuries there has been legitimate curiosity about the years during which the young aspirant to religious life moves from the status of neophyte to full-fledged sister. A mysterious aura, subject to variations of interpretation, surrounds the training period and particularly the canonical year of the enclosed novitiate. Actually, there is nothing essentially secret about the objective process by which Marjorie Heath becomes Sister Mary Joan, but the truly personal aspects of the ascetical experience have made it difficult to describe, even when the novice so desires. While it would be false to say that the introductory period bears any resemblance to the mystical state which St. Teresa and St. John of the Cross had such difficulty in describing, it is true that the deepened sense of commitment, the increased periods given to theological studies and ascetical reading, the training in both liturgical and personal prayer combine to make the young religious self-consciously aware that the most important parts of her formation period cannot be communicated. This, of course, is equally true of any deeply felt human experience, one Edgar Lee Masters describes so effectively in "Silence," when he has the old soldier explain his amputated leg to the questioning boy with, "A bear bit it off," because, as Masters continues,

   . . . if he could describe it all
he would be an artist.

But if he were an artist there would be deeper wounds which he could not describe.

The formal aspects of the period of training which, since the promulgation of the revised code of canon law in 1917, had been until Vatican II basically the same for all congregations of women include the postulancy, the period of probation preliminary to the taking of the habit, the novitiate which begins with the reception of the habit, the period which has as its object, "the forming of the mind of the novice by means of the study of the rule and constitutions, by pious meditations and assiduous prayer, by instruction on those matters which pertain to the vows and the virtues, by suitable exercises in rooting out the germs of vice, in regulating the motives of the soul, in acquiring virtues" (Canon 565 #1), and the juniorate, that period after the first profession of temporary vows during which the young religious receives further training in religious life and professional training for the specific apostolate in which she will be engaged.

The nineteenth-century religious frequently did not complete the training period but, like her secular sister, pioneered in areas and filled positions which today would be occupied only by professionally qualified personnel. In the current criticism of the Catholic education of the past it is easy to overemphasize this fact and to forget that the free public school was also staffed by young men and women whose educational attainments might be little more than those of the children they taught. Ralph Waldo Emerson at fourteen was a country schoolteacher saving his money to attend Harvard. Walt Whitman, whose formal education never went beyond six grades, taught school as he himself says "up and down New York state." Qualifying teachers' examinations in many states were given annually to high school seniors as late as the first decades of the twentieth century, with interested seniors given released time from public high school to enable them to attend preparatory educational courses in normal schools when proximity made this feasible. Awareness of the need for improvement of the present structures in the Church need not be prefaced by exaggerated breast striking over the inadequacies of the past.

In 1917 the revised code of canon law made the training period of postulancy and novitiate a requirement for all religious orders, with a more formal structure of spiritual and professional preparation evolving. The problems incident to the drawing up of a formation program arise from a multiplicity of causes. Unlike trainees for other programs, the novice is being prepared for a way of life, for what Joseph H. Fichter calls "the whole system of cultural and social patterns that make up the expected behavior of a full-time religious functionary," [1] and at the same time is being given the academic preparation necessary for the professional area in which her apostolic vocation will lie. This naturally constitutes one of the knottiest problems in the construction of the training program, for although those in charge of the formation of the young religious realize that they are dealing with a whole person, an ambiguity of emphasis is bound to occur. The ascetical does not necessarily exclude the practical, but the beginner in any field lacks experience which enables her to evaluate things in their proper order. Each new learning experience achieves an importance out of all proportion to its place in the over-all pattern. It is difficult for the beginner to achieve the spiritual poise and balance that recognize professional excellence as a *sine qua non* for achievement in God's service with the equally valid proposition that without him she can do nothing.

The traditional emphasis in the novitiates of the past upon the virtues associated with community living tended to place undue emphasis upon docility, conformity, the dignity of all work, and silence, emphasis which, while not expressly downgrading scholastic excellence and productivity, appeared to underrate their effective place in the service of God. Anonymity was preferred to publicity, and humility was linked to the unnoticed, routine mental tasks—an administrator might be "brilliant," but the lay brother was always "humble." Today the pendulum is in danger of swinging in the opposite direction. Today's young religious is aware from the day she takes the pre-entrance aptitude tests that she will be expected to develop her potential to its full capacity for professional performance of the various general and specialized works of the institute. She will be given opportunities to study and to make actual in her own life the spiritual realities in the paradox of God's so loving the world as to give his only begotten son for its salvation, and that son's own prayer that was not for the world; she will take courses in public speaking while she learns the spiritual resources of silence; and she will be encouraged to question her motives in obedience.

It is a period which is essentially one of trial, during which the congregation tests the individual's aptitude for the life of the community, and the novice in turn decides whether this is truly the life to which God calls her, evaluates this congregation, this apostolate in the context of her total dedication.

In this respect the essential reason for the formation period has not changed from the earlier periods in which the two-way process of getting acquainted frequently took place in the actual experience of living and working in one of the smaller houses. While there were obvious weaknesses in introducing the neophyte immediately to the work of the congregation there were also advantages. She was inducted experientially into the traditions of the congregation, that ephemeral but very real spirit which differentiates the numerous congregations in the Church joined by their common dedication, identical consecration, and similarity of apostolic objective. The spirit of community with its distinctive focus is rarely learned from books, not even from the biographies and writings of the founder; it is translated into reality by the lives of the members who, like members of a family, have a clear if undefinable resemblance to each other. The young religious of an earlier era was also placed immediately into contact with those whom she would serve for the remainder of her life, a contact which kept her continually aware of the purpose of her vocation.

Even professional training was not as inadequate as a similar program would prove today. The young religious worked with an experienced teacher or nurse who herself less torn by multiple extraprofessional involvements had time to give to her young trainee. As the twentieth-century world became more complex, the body of learning more vast, it was obvious that such a casual induction into religious life and its professional commitments was woefully insufficient. Many congregations had been aware of the increasing sophistication of the world in which their sisters would work, and had been making valiant efforts to prepare them both spiritually and professionally. The first Catholic college for women, Notre Dame of Maryland, received a charter from the state of Maryland on April 2, 1896, authorizing the conferring of degrees, and sisters on the faculty attended the Catholic University of America's newly opened graduate school. Other Catholic colleges for women sprang up across the country, and growing numbers of sisters attended these and the universities which had begun to accept women, particularly during the summer session when the religious were free to attend.

The upward economic mobility of the Catholic population, together with the complexity of the contemporary world, made it increasingly obvious that, however valiantly individual congregations were working to provide members with training for their work in hospitals and schools, the growing criticism that many young religious did not have sufficient training or maturity for the role alloted to them was only too valid.

In September 1951, Pope Pius XII gave his epochal address to the First International Congress of Teaching Sisters in Rome, warning of the dangers inherent in this state. Said the Holy Father, "Many of your schools are praised and described to us as very good—but not all. It is our fervent wish that all strive to become excellent. This presupposes that your teaching sisters are masters of the subjects they expound. See to it, therefore, that they are well trained, and that their education corresponds in quality and academic degrees to that demanded by the state. Be generous in giving them all they need, especially where books are concerned, so that they may continue their studies, and thus offer young people a rich and solid harvest of knowledge.

This is in keeping with the Catholic idea which gratefully welcomes all that is naturally good, beautiful, and true, because it is an image of the Divine goodness, beauty, and truth. Most parents entrust their daughters to you because their consciences bid them do so. But this does not mean that the children should suffer by receiving in your schools an education of inferior value. On the contrary, you must do all that you can to assure parents that their children are getting the best education from the very elementary classes on. And then, do not forget that knowledge and good teaching win the respect and consideration of the children for the teaching sister. Thus she can exercise greater influence on their character and spiritual life." [2]

A year later the Pope gave another address to a meeting of superiors general of women's religious communities in Rome, at which time he repeated his earlier recommendations for the formation of sisters, and went even further by saying, "Be it a question of education, pedagogy, the care of the sick, artistic or other activities, the sister should entertain the conviction: 'My superior is making possible for me a formation that will put me on equal footing with my colleagues in the world.' Make it possible for them, and give them the means to keep their professional knowledge and training up to date. On this point we have also elaborated during the past year. We repeat it in order to underscore the importance of this requirement for the interior peace and for the work of your sisters." [3]

Fortified by these two directives, and under the inspired leadership of Sister Mary Emil, IHM, Marygrove College, Detroit, the Sister Formation Conference, which many have called one of the most significant developments in Catholic education in the United States, was born. As a member of the College and University Department of the National Catholic Educational Association, the conference grew out of a meeting of the Teacher Education section at the 1952 convention in Kansas City and regional meetings of major superiors and sisters in intellectual and spiritual formation positions during 1953.

In the years which followed, Sister Mary Emil, accompanied by one of her sisters, or by Sister Ritamary, CHM, Ottumwa Heights College, Ottumwa, Iowa, cofounder of the conference, toured the United States, traveling thousands of miles and visiting almost every mother house in the country. One drove, the other kept correspondence up to date on a portable typewriter.[4] With quiet and steady purpose, the conference accumulated pertinent data concerning the training of the teaching sisters in the United States, evoked from bishops, priests, educators, and sisters intense and reflective thinking about the training program, its inadequacies, the effects of the inadequacies, and the possible remedying of a frankly undesirable situation. Questionnaires sent to 377 general superiors of the teaching communities in the United States revealed that, although religious communities agreed that a four-year college program leading to a bachelor's degree is basic and a fifth year of graduate specialization ideal for all sisters before they are assigned to teach in a classroom, only thirteen communities out of the 255 which responded to the questionnaire had a full bachelor's degree program in operation.[5]

"One hundred and eighteen communities had neither educational facilities of their own for the training of their subjects, nor easy access to those of suitable Catholic colleges and universities," [6] reported Sister Mary Emil in her introduction to *The Mind of the Church in the Formation of Sisters.* The early studies indicated that something had to be done to prepare the sisters for the modern apostolate which, as the Pope had pointed out, required one who could face boldly the gigantic tasks of the age, one able to meet its dangers, overcome its spiritual destitution, competent to think for himself, and formed to maturity of judgment.[7]

The problems of implementing such a program were incredibly complex. Pastors already aware of a sister "shortage" were reluctant to see that number reduced still more by the postponement of the young religious' entrance into the active apostolate by the proposed lengthening of her preparation. The assurance that the hardship, while acute, would be only temporary, that when the first group of "formation" sisters entered the schools equipped with their degrees the flow of teachers would continue uninterruptedly was no comfort to the hard-pressed administrators forced to deal with the immediate problem. The necessity of replacing the missing sisters with lay teachers to whom in justice an adequate living wage had to be paid pointed up the inadequacies of the sisters' stipends. In many cases the salaries of the sisters did not cover living expenses. The care of the infirm and retired and the education of the young religious made a more realistic salary scale mandatory. While harassed community treasurers still try to match debit with credit, the gap between the sisters' monthly check and current living costs is considerably less than it was a dozen years ago. School boards have faced the problem and are still struggling with it—and while the going has not always been smooth, the majority of dioceses have accepted the Sister Formation program as a reality and have made whatever personal adjustments were necessary.

Mother Thomas Aquinas Carroll, RSM, has summarized the magnitude of change involved in implementing the conviction that the sister should complete her undergraduate studies on a full-time basis in an environment which would aid her in integrating intellectual, cultural, and professional life with spiritual and apostolic growth.

Colleges with satisfactory programs had to be found or founded, faculty prepared, residences built: thousands of classrooms in parochial schools substituted secular teachers for the expected young religious; new forms of doctrinal instruction and of apostolic involvement had to be worked out; most importantly, former ways of proceeding and standards of professional conduct had to be critically reviewed and often repudiated.[8]

That the effort, sacrifice, and work which accompanied this program have reaped abundant fruit is evidenced in a recent report of a study conducted by Sister M. Brideen Long, OSF, president of Holy Family College, Manitowoc, Wisconsin.[9]

In 1952 Sister Brideen conducted an investigation to determine to what extent the pre-service education of Catholic elementary-school teachers prepared them for the teaching tasks of the elementary school. Data were secured from questionnaires and interviews with 1800 sisters, representing 200 different religious communities, who began to teach between 1941 and 1951. Returns were received from 76.5 percent of the sisters contacted and revealed what concerned Catholic educators had suspected, that the period of pre-service education was too short to prepare the teachers adequately for the teaching tasks assigned them.

In the summer of 1965 Sister sent 2000 questionnaires to 200 Catholic colleges in which undergraduate and graduate sisters were enrolled. The questionnaire, the same one used in 1952, was distributed to sisters who had taught at least one year but no longer than ten years. Replies were received from 1286 sisters, members of 225 religious communities, or 64.3 percent of the number contacted.

The purpose of the investigation, which was to show the progress that religious communities have made in the last decade in the preparation of teachers for the elementary schools, and indirectly to bring out the influence of the Sister Formation movement, has obviously been achieved. Analysis of the data seemed to Sister Brideen to warrant the conclusion that the length of pre-service preparation has definitely increased within the past decade; "the percentage of participating Sisters holding a degree before beginning to teach increased from 7.1 percent in 1955 to 41.9 percent in 1964. The number having at least 3 years of pre-service preparation increased from 9.2 percent to 38.0 percent." [10]

These encouraging statistics are evidence of the wisdom, the foresight, and the courage of the early leaders in the Sister Formation movement. Member communities were encouraged to share their educational resources through interchange of college instructors, of especially prepared experts in various fields, of outstanding speakers and programs, libraries, laboratories, and by the establishment of houses of studies on college campuses so that sisters of smaller congregations might enjoy community life while pursuing their studies away from the mother house.

The Everett curriculum, a master plan for sister education, while flexible enough to permit adaptation to local circumstances, has been for many of the religious community colleges a guiding program for the integrating of spiritual with intellectual formation. The curriculum took its name from Everett, Washington, in which, during the summer of 1956, Ph.D.s from seventeen Catholic women's colleges, each an expert in a different academic field, met to devise an "ideal" college curriculum for young sisters in training to be teachers, nurses, and social workers. Supported by a grant from the Ford Foundation Fund for the Advancement of Education, these eminent sister educators, together with twelve part-time consultants, spent the three months discussing, studying, and writing a curricular proposal for a five-year collegiate education of sisters.[11] As Sister Emil noted in her report on the Workshop (NCEA College *Newsletter,* XX (January 1957), pp. 6–9) the Everett curriculum emphasizes liberal education, and by correlation of theology and philosophy, an emphasis on methodological and conceptual unity enables young nun teachers, nurses, social workers, and catechists to be given basically the same liberal arts formation. Specialization is relegated to the last quarter of the five-year program.

The really distinguishing mark of both the Everett curriculum and its various modifications, the characteristic which differentiates the training of the sister from that of any student in a liberal arts program pursued in any undergraduate college, is its unification. There is a gradual and progressive introduction into the threefold aspect of vocation, the academic, the ascetical, and the apostolic. While no one of these is to be considered in isolation, a focus of attention on the individual areas during the various periods of training permits concentration on each aspect. Sister Formation personnel have themselves received guidance from the various publications of the conference: *The Sister Formation Bulletin,* a quarterly now in its ninth year, various special communications sent out by the executive secretary, reprint circulation, world-wide correspondence, and the six-volume Sister Formation Series, the proceedings of the biannual regional conferences published by Fordham University Press. A significant factor in the religious-apostolic

emphasis in the formation programs has been the annual
Institute of Spirituality conducted by Rev. Elio Gambari,
SMM, of the Sacred Congregation, Rome, for the directresses
of the three formation groups. Father Gambari's *Syllabus of
Spirituality*, an adaptation for religious women of the guidelines set forth in *Sedes Sapientia*, emphasizes the formation
of the Christian person during the postulate in preparation
for the ascetical formation of the novitiate, which will be
followed by the apostolic formation during the juniorate.
On all three levels the academic, cultural, psychological, and
physical aspects of the program of formation run parallel to
the spiritual formation, with the latter always taking preced-
ence.

While a certain gratification over what has been accomplished in an incredibly short time is justifiable, neither
Sister Formation leaders nor the conference of major superiors of which, since 1964, Sister Formation has become a
committee have ever permitted themselves that luxury.
Courageous self-criticism and honest self-evaluation have
been and continue to be a germinating force. In 1965 Sister
Grace Miriam, assistant executive secretary of SFC, conducted
a survey and presented a pre-service report on the education
of sisters for the major superiors, a report which corroborated
Sister Brideen's findings, that while much had been accomplished, a small but significant sector was beneath the
national level in the pre-service training of the young religious. Recommendations paralleling those of Sister Brideen
have been drawn up, urging smaller religious communities
to seek co-operation with a firmly established college of
another religious community, and agreeing with Sister Rose
Dominic, executive secretary of SFC, who cautions religious
communities against starting a college without sufficient
enrollment, well-qualified faculty, adequate library and
equipment, and the possibility of regional accreditation
within a short time.[12]

An on-going special committee consisting of sister educators who had been at Everett, sister educators who had
emerged into the forefront of Sister Formation more recently,
and some directors of formation under the chairmanship of

Mother Thomas Aquinas Carroll, RSM, has prepared a position paper to serve as a base for curricular study of what sisters may need educationally in the next ten years. The paper lists matters to be considered as: the extent to which Sister Formation principles implicit in the Everett curriculum have been implemented; the problems which have evolved in the application of the Everett guidelines; the limitations of a program planned in 1956 for the decade of 1966; and new proposals to meet the new situation.

The committee is keenly aware of the changes both in the world and in the Church, and the obligations these changes impose upon all those entrusted with the preparation of young religious to make whatever adjustments in the program the times require. While not presuming to anticipate the decisions of the investigating committee, one might hazard a guess that the curricula of the future will place greater emphasis upon the social science sequence, earlier introduction, if only on a part-time basis, into the social apostolate, and the life of the congregation as lived in the local houses. Individual communities have already been experimenting in these directions. Sisters in the Juniorate of the Sisters of the Holy Cross, Notre Dame, Indiana, are hostesses for high school retreats which are held approximately every six weeks, and for the children of South Bend's Peter Claver House. Postulants of the Sisters of Notre Dame of Namur assist teachers in the Washington public schools; Chicago's Cabrini project had Franciscan junior sisters from Winona, Minnesota, serving in the summer program; the Missionary Servants of the Most Blessed Trinity find it helpful to have their postulants visit and fill part-time assignments in the charity offices and catechetical centers; the Sisters of Charity of St. Vincent de Paul have their candidates work in different areas of the city, mingling with people in depressed areas, working in city playgrounds. Postulants and junior sisters of the School Sisters of Notre Dame participate in CCD and in Operation Head Start as aides to the professional workers, activities which give meaning to their academic studies dealing with problems of human responsibility.

Efforts are also being made to give the young religious

some experience of life away from the mother house and the peer group by sending them for brief periods of time, usually during the interterm break and during the summer, to nearby convents where they participate in the life and work of the house. Superiors realize that the apostolic orientation of the Church in America not only permits the religious to participate in institutional systems other than the religious, but even demands that the person so participating must achieve the technical excellence shared by secular persons.

Whatever adjustments result from the post-conciliar self-study in which each congregation is currently engaged, the training of the young members will, one suspects, continue to follow the general guidelines of the Sister Formation Conference. Whatever shifts of emphasis in these seem desirable, the aims will remain those given in the March 1955 *Sister Formation Bulletin*, "to produce the sister teacher (or hospital or social worker) with integrated personality, who regards professional preparation as part of a way of life in reaching sanctity, and a life of sanctity as the framework into which specialization fits naturally and without ostentation."

NINE

After Vatican II

After the opening of Montreal's fair on April 28, 1967, Pierre Dupuy, commissioner general of Expo 67 said, "Whether he knows it or not, whether it pleases him or not, man is swept up in a huge wave of change which is transforming before his very eyes continents and peoples." [1] This statement, with minor adaptations, might well be a summary of what is happening within the Church, and particularly within that special segment of the Church, religious life. It is impossible, as I have emphasized repeatedly throughout this book, to make any definitive statement concerning these changes which would be accepted by all religious congregations. What might represent radical adaptation in some areas might have been the time-honored custom in others.

This past week, for example, newspapers carried an interesting feature story of a young Divine Savior sister who during the summer will temporarily don lay clothes in order to gain experience as a journalist with a large metropolitan newspaper. This wearing of lay clothes in a professional milieu has long been the custom of the Columban sisters studying medicine in Dublin, a congregation which at this writing still wears the religious habit within the convent and when engaged in direct missionary works of the apostolate. Examples of this type of new-old can be multiplied, and will increase rather than lessen as general chapters meet for the all-important business of examining their life and work in the light of contemporary needs.

Fortunately, the direction the adaptation will take does not depend upon arbitrary factors, such as whether the congregation is composed of avid readers of *The Wanderer* or *The National Catholic Reporter*. Throughout the sixteen documents of Vatican II there are references to the role of the religious in the modern world, and in addition there are the directives in Chapter VI of *Lumen Gentium,* as well as in the ground plan for the appropriate renewal of religious life laid out in *Perfectae Caritatis.* In these two documents, and in the special Norms of August 1966, chapters of religious women have an outline for their self-study and the pattern for debate and discussion on whatever updating seems mandatory. The specific form this renovating will take in each institute is still very open, but the area for dialogue is clearly marked. Whatever decisions are made, they will be the outcome of study, thought, discussion, and experimentation by the entire congregation.

That the wishes of the Council fathers may not suffer from delaying tactics on the part of more traditionally oriented communities which might have felt satisfied with the *status quo,* the Holy See has specified that "a special general chapter should be convened within two or, at most, three years to promote adaptation and renewal in each institute." [2]

Preparation for this general chapter differs in each congregation, but the involvement of all members is universal. Smaller congregations have held "little councils," during which a systematic study of the relative Council documents and of the congregation's rule, constitution, and customs in relation to these documents is made. Larger congregations have distributed suggested outlines by which local communities might conduct similar studies, after which regional meetings are held, during which, ideas of all members are pooled, suggestions weighed, areas of experimentation explored. A third method, also conducted on the local level, concludes with written reports, summarized by a regional chairman and submitted to the members of the chapter. In order to ascertain the wishes of the sisters some congregations have asked for suggestions, have sponsored provincial polls, elected *ad hoc* committees to draw up proposals which are then submitted to the total religious body for approval or rejection. Others have invited theologians, sociologists, cultural leaders, and experts in related fields to speak at workshops and study days, at which sisters of one congregation or of several have gathered to discuss areas of common interest and crucial problems of contemporary religious life. The sisters are not only making plans for the future; they are engaged in a serious self-study to enable them to get a clear picture of both weaknesses and strengths in the present, a knowledge essential if the projected changes are to be both daring and prudent.

The election of chapter delegates has never been conducted according to a single plan, and this variation is certain to become even more pronounced as congregations attempt to adjust the system to assure a democratic representation. Very small congregations may find it is feasible to have direct balloting of all eligible members, that is, all those who have taken vows. Larger groups may decide upon representation by region, by age grouping, by work areas, or by simple selection of the chapter sisters from a complete list of all professed sisters. Each method has its advantages and its weaknesses, and the pre-chapter committees are engaged in adaptations which will increase the former while minimizing the latter.

When chapter delegates have been elected, the sisters whom they represent are invited to make known their wishes and to submit suggestions, and chapter delegates are urged to make a serious study not only of the traditions of their own congregation and the expressed wishes of the members, but of all documents of Vatican II and the contemporary needs of society. They are aware of their responsibility not only to those they represent, but to the entire people of God, not only to the living present, but to the yet unborn future. With automation experts warning us that the high school student now making long-range plans for his future lifework will need retraining at least five times before he retires, no congregation can risk drawing up plans for a frozen structure which will require fundamental revision at frequent intervals. The bases of adaptation will have to be broad enough to admit of shift in non-essential areas, flexible enough to permit the dropping of elements which upon trial prove to be unrealistic or impractical. The chapter sisters are asked to face boldly the gigantic tasks of the present age, to foresee the problems of the future, and through intelligent and open-minded discussion form judgments upon which the congregation can build its future.

Perfectae Caritatis recommends that chapters . . . "faithfully acquit themselves of the governing role given them; each should express in its own way the fact that all members of the community have a share in the welfare of the whole community and a responsibility for it" (#14).

This involvement of all the members of the work of renewal serves as a balancing force, restraining the too-eager and impelling the complacent, forcing both groups to a re-examination of principles upon which religious life rests.

Both *Lumen Gentium* and *Perfectae Caritatis* emphasize the links that join today to yesterday, the former by stressing the fact that communities "grow and flourish in accord with the spirit of their founders" (#45), and the latter by pointing out that the appropriate renewal of religious life involves two simultaneous processes: (1) a continuous return to the sources of all Christian life and to the original inspiration behind a given community and (2) an adjustment of the community to the changed conditions of the times (#2).

An amusing aspect of this twofold directive is the fact that for many religious congregations, arriving at agreement regarding the charismatic gift of the founder, which is the authentic spirit of the order, is more difficult than an assessment of the crying needs of the contemporary world. History and a sometimes too admiring hagiographer have dimmed the realities which confronted the founder, and softened the human problems with which he struggled. As the works in which he pioneered became formalized and fitted to a later society's pattern, his prophetic vision and daring were blurred. Social activity uniquely creative in his generation may have become standardized in ours, and an unquestioning acceptance of the work itself as the spirit of the congregation might today be a barrier to progress that the founder would be the first to break.

For some congregations a confrontation with their founders may well result in the burning of bridges, a raw courage for the twentieth-century nuns that will match the fortitude of earlier ages. For others (and while I cannot foretell the future I venture to guess this may be the road my own congregation will take) it will be a redefining of the terms of the commitment. While education will probably remain the primary objective of the School Sisters of Notre Dame, I am reasonably sure that its definition will be expanded to include all the overtones in the more connotative sense of the word. That the apostolic horizons of the sisters will be enlarged as a result is evident from the multiple educational works in which we are already engaged, work undreamed of a decade ago.

Some of the problems with which the chapters will deal are similar .to those with which the Council fathers wrestled. The problem of authority must be considered, particularly in relation to subsidiarity. The hierarchical structure built upon the ecclesiastical model of Pope-bishop-priest-layman will undoubtedly come under consideration, and in many instances undergo a complete modification. While larger world-wide congregations may find it necessary to retain central administrative offices whose responsibility will be the co-ordination of apostolic works of the entire community, both provincial and local superiors will be empowered to make many more judgments within their geographical area without recourse to this higher authority. The norms for adaptation specifically state that "superiors on every level should be given sufficient powers so that useless and too frequent recourse to higher authorities does not increase" (#18). Some congregations are experimenting with a rotating pattern of administration; others have local houses to which no superior has been assigned, decisions for the group being decided through group discussion and vote. The

majority, which retain the traditional superior, are emphasizing her charismatic role.

The six regional meetings during 1966–67 of the Sister
Formation Conference focused upon the local superior and
her role, specifically on her role as the last member of the
formation personnel. Additional diocesan meetings dealing
with related aspects of the local superior and her place in
the structure of contemporary religious life have been held;
Spiritual Institutes have given the sisters themselves opportunity to discuss the relationship of the superior with her
sisters, a position increasingly recognized as that of "first
among peers." Several congregations have held workshops
for local superiors before or shortly after their appointment
to office, so that the superiors themselves may benefit from
group study, lectures, and dialogue, and in some cases these
workshops have been composed of all the congregations in
the geographic area. The objective in all these sessions is to
make sure that the superior sees her assignment as an opportunity to promote consensus, a genuine thinking, feeling,
and willing together of all the sisters.

The whole question of corporate and individual poverty
is being re-examined, and the legal distinctions between the
vow and virtue, which unconsciously bred some of the more
obvious inconsistencies, have become less important than the
contemporary interpretation of the beatitude and its implications in a socially conscious century increasingly aware of
the rapidly widening gap between the affluent two-car, multi-
level-ranch-house middle class and the unemployed slum
dweller in his rat-infested tenement.

Canon law, an area of church legislation a previous generation of sisters was content to leave completely in the hands
of men trained in the fine distinctions of language, is, during
this post-conciliar period, being studied seriously by a committee of religious superiors of women concerned about its
practical application to the psychological needs of women.
They plan to submit their recommendations to the ecclesiastical commission assigned the task of drawing up the new
code, procedure which will, for the first time in a good many

centuries, recognize the fact that laws for men are not suitable for women.

Courses of study in the period of formation are undergoing revision to permit greater emphasis upon the study of Scripture, particularly the Gospels, since, as *Perfectae Caritatis* points out, "the fundamental norm of the religious life is a following of Christ as proposed by the gospel" (#2). In addition, classes in theology, Scripture, and liturgy are offered in an increasing number of centers so that sisters whose professional commitment permits them only a limited time may also have opportunity to become acquainted with recent thinking in these areas. These in-service courses frequently offered during regular summer school sessions have the added advantage of bringing sisters of many communities together, and in some instances, as in the programs at Loyola University, Chicago, in which laymen are also enrolled, of emphasizing the community aspect of the whole people of God.

In answer to the Council's recommendation that all communities should participate in the life of the church, fostering in every possible way her scriptural, liturgical, doctrinal, pastoral, ecumenical, missionary, and social enterprises,[3] religious are being encouraged to participate specifically in ways that would have been considered incredible less than a dozen years ago. One hears of parishes where sisters and pastor team-teach convert groups, or where the sisters' casual parish visiting serves to alert the priest to specific needs.

America [4] recently carried an article on the work of the nuns in Brazil, a country with a population of 4 million with only 12,000 priests to serve its people. In 1963 Bishop Eugenio de Araujo Sales, then apostolic administrator of Natal, turned to Brazil's 40,000 nuns and appointed Mother Irany Bastos, of the Congregation of Jesus Crucified, administrator of the Nisia Floresta parish in Rio Grande del Norte. Today ten parishes in Brazil have been placed under sister administrators, and it is expected that by the end of the current year that figure will have doubled. The ministries performed by the sisters include distributing Holy Com-

munion, baptizing, preparing couples for marriage, assisting
the dying, and delivering sermons at Masses.

Whether American parishioners will hear a sister preach
from the parish pulpit as Sister Adelheid, osb, did in St.
Theresa's Church, Klagenfurt, Austria, on World Prayer
Sunday 1967, remains hidden in the future,[5] but in less
formal situations the American nun has been given opportunities to address not only the laity, but priests and semi-
narians. There are even a few sisters teaching in seminaries,
and their number will undoubtedly increase as seminaries,
like other Catholic colleges, share facilities and faculties.

In Jersey City more than two dozen nuns from several
congregations teach in a novel ccd school held at All Saints
parish. Directed to non-Catholic children in an inner city,
the school is concerned with more than religious instruction;
classes try to meet the communication needs of the children.
The school is an outgrowth of a summer program conducted
in the area with the help of antipoverty funds.

The ecumenical recommendations of the Council fell upon
particularly receptive ears in religious congregations of
women, for they have been making gestures in that direction
for some time. The extent to which they have responded
specifically remains, of course, dependent upon the climate
of the area in which they are situated. One of the speakers
at the 1966 Sisters Spiritual Institute in San Antonio was
Rabbi Arthur Gilbert. The 1966 Sister Formation-sponsored
summer workshop at Marquette University had as its theme
the three ecumenisms of nation, of race, of faith. Interfaith
weeks on college campuses have become routine, consistently
well-attended activities of the scholastic calendar. At my own
college during the past year students have heard Pastor Max
Lachman; Rabbi Henry B. Pastor, who in addition to speaking to an all-school assembly on Jewish holidays and ceremonies was guest lecturer in theology and sociology classes;
Pastor Lowell Mays, one of the auditors at Vatican II representing American Lutherans; John Stergiardes, cantor at
Annunciation Greek Orthodox Church. Students collaborated
in an Interfaith Sacred concert with choirs from Temple
Shalom, Mount Carmel Lutheran, and sixteen young adults

from Padon Baptist Church. Sisters were invited to and attended the dinner honoring Dr. Latourette of Yale Theological School, at Concordia Lutheran Seminary, a situation which the honor guest noted as impossible ten years ago. Courses in comparative religion are incorporated into theology department offerings, and leaders of non-Catholic faiths give courses in Scripture and the history of the Church in several large Catholic universities, with reciprocal arrangements for visiting Roman Catholic professors.

When St. James' new parochial school in Madison, Wisconsin, was not completed in time for the opening of classes, Rabbi Lipshitz, with the approval of his board of directors and people offered their synagogue school, Beth Israel Center, for as long a time as it might be needed. In Milwaukee, Wisconsin, when a gas-main explosion partially destroyed a new parochial school, a nearby Methodist church offered its facilities.

When the history of Christ Church, Mequon, Wisconsin, is written, it will be noted that during the early days of its formation, this congregation of the Lutheran Church in America held Sunday services at a Roman Catholic convent, Notre Dame of the Lake, mother house of the School Sisters of Notre Dame. With the permission of Archbishop William E. Cousins of Milwaukee, the choral room, "made to order," with its tiered seating, electric organ, and piano, was turned over to Pastor Danielson and his congregation when they found themselves without a church until the materialization of their building plans. The comments of a neighboring Lutheran pastor, Rev. O. V. Anderson, are significant, "Never before have dedicated nuns ushered Lutherans to worship. Marvelous things are happening in our day." [6]

The prayer life of the post-conciliar nun is also undergoing change. Liturgically centered and in the vernacular as it has not been for centuries, longer time for mental prayer is replacing the litanies, the devotional vocal prayers which over the centuries were compensation for the recitation of the Office which, since it was said in Latin, remained, for many, more of a penitential practice than an encounter with God. (For an excellent historical summary of prayer in

religious orders see *Nuns, Community Prayer and Change.*[7])
The breviary itself, according to the revisions listed in the
Constitution on the Sacred Liturgy (#88–89; 101) has been
restored to its original importance as "a source of piety
and nourishment for personal prayer" (*Sacred Liturgy* #90).
Time-honored horaria are currently being adjusted, not only
to make the sisters available to those they serve at times
convenient for them, but also so that the hours of Lauds and
Vespers, as well as Compline and the Little Hour, which are
said privately, might be celebrated at a time consistent with
the theme of the hour. This directive is emphasized by the
constitution, which says, "That the day may be truly sancti-
fied, and that the hours themselves may be recited with
spiritual advantage, it is best that each of them be prayed at
a time which most closely corresponds with its true canonical
time" (#94).

This aspect of religious life, as well as renewed emphasis
on the Mass as the focus of prayer life, is the consideration
of congregations engaged in renewal. In fact, many are following the recommendations of Father Bernard Häring that
there must not only be legislation as to the prayer life, but
also that the whole rule and constitution be tested in this
perspective, namely, whether such legislation helps to unify
life in prayer and in the Eucharist.[8]

Many congregations following Cardinal Suenens' recommendation for more "candor and openness between nuns,
more mutual sincerity, more real sharing, constructive self-
criticism in common, with a view towards closer co-operation
in the accomplishment of their great mission" [9] have
adopted the procedures of group dynamics for examination
and correction of faults or the focusing on an apostolate in
a common situation, an exercise which serves to increase
self-knowledge and to encourage generosity in community
effort.

Adjustment of the horaria to the needs of the local convent
is being adopted by an increasing number of congregations,
and in many, mental prayer, a non-communal exercise, is
left to the individual sister's convenience both in regard to
place and to time, although the minimum length of time

devoted to this exercise is usually set down in the constitution. Spontaneous prayer is encouraged, the bidding prayers of the Mass providing many with a liturgical introduction
to this increasingly popular form of gratitude and petition.
In general, community prayers are becoming more Church-
centered, while responsibility for them is becoming more
personal.

Spiritual reading, for which St. Benedict provided in the
fifth century and which all congregations since have considered an essential prelude to prayer, particularly mental
prayer, has, with the recent improvement in quality books,
played an increasingly important role in the sister's ascetical
and apostolic life. Few sisters have not read the contemporary giants: Fathers Schillebeeckx, Weigel, Häring, both
Rahners, Ahern, Murray, Goldbrunner, Van Kaam, and
Merton. And while the number of those who are familiar
with Barth and Bonhoefer, Marty and Buber will be considerably less, there is increased awareness of the trend in
the socially oriented theology outside the Church. Convent
libraries have come a long way from the "born-holy-and-
never-got-over-it" lives of the saints of an earlier generation.
Some religious have established community lending libraries
so that smaller houses financially unable to buy books may
have the benefit of the best of current authors. Catechetical
curriculum libraries are set up in many mother houses, and
those engaged in this work, either full or part time, are free
to use the libraries and the teaching aids. The Jerusalem
Bible, or the Anchor edition, is in the pews of convent
chapels almost more than in convent libraries, for the
sisters' use of Scripture is as much prayerful as it is scholarly.
Novenas are few and far between, and attendance at these in
most communities is a matter of choice.

In the reassessment of the time-honored practices of mortification, congregations are dropping those which have no
meaning for the young woman of today and those which
seem incompatible with the specific apostolate in which they
are engaged. Detailed regulations regarding food and fasting
have been dropped in favor of a more personal approach to
penance. Mortification has not been dropped; the words of

Christ are as valid for the Christian of today as for those who followed him in Galilee. Unless we do penance we shall all likewise perish. But the post-Vatican II religious, engaged as she is in many activities both within and without the convent, frequently finds her mortification the inevitable corollary of the work. The willingness to accept a job and the steadfastness needed to carry it through to completion are in themselves a mortification, especially if she can make the small added sacrifice of not talking about the difficulties she finds in the work.

The "spiritual nosegays" of retreat manuals and meditation books of an earlier age seem slightly artificial to the realistic young woman of today; for her, penance grows out of the apostolate, out of tensions of contemporary life, out of the inevitable adjustment of individual to group. However, the religious of today is aware, as was her predecessor, that love is not love if it is not paid for in personal gift, in sacrifice. The mother may not dramatize her gift giving as sacrifice, but when the child is born, so is a mother with all the word connotes. In a similar fashion the young woman who takes vows adds something to her personality, something which will germinate in an awareness of the needs of others and an eagerness to serve them. St. Francis de Sales' motto, "Ask for nothing, refuse nothing," can make demands upon the sister who adopts it which no program of planned mortification can equal. A novice told me recently that a resolution to say yes to every reasonable request on one day a week called for as much generosity as she could muster, and those who judge her a selfish young woman might test themselves in the same program. To the nun of today there is something slightly self-conscious, spiritually speaking, about working at mortification; she much prefers to work at service, at acts that flow from love. The mortification will inevitably follow. If she can choose the work, anticipating the difficulties, she has accepted the mortification Christ himself chooses for her. It is, perhaps, this type of self-imposed suffering to which the Norms refer in suggesting that religious should adopt new forms of penance and mortification, "drawn from the modern conditions of life." [10]

In the chapter on poverty I have discussed both its meaning for the individual religious and the means congregations are taking to insure that the recommendations of *Perfectae Caritatis* (#13) be incorporated into the lives of the sisters. It might not be entirely repetitious, however, to point out that both in matter of personal poverty embraced in imitation of Christ and that of corporate witness, religious are seriously examining areas in which changes can be made. In a highly sophisticated civilization, professional training is an essential element for those who would serve others, and professional training is a long, tedious, and expensive process. To suggest that the aspirant to religious life should have already completed this training would be to discriminate (in the name of poverty!) against those whose financial status would prevent their obtaining it.

While the recent well-publicized assets of one or another congregation were ironic gloss to their non-profit-making status, much so-called wealth is tied up in property acquired at a time when squatters' rights were sufficient to assure ownership, and in hospitals, schools, homes for the aged, whose income balances expenditures only because those entrusted with their administration keep a close watch on both and make few personal demands. This is not to say that the building binge, which religious congregations experienced in common with an America that expanded more rapidly in the past quarter century than in its whole previous history, was in itself a good thing. The future may well see a tendency for religious women to live in smaller convents, as it will see the erection of smaller churches for smaller parishes. Already some communities that find themselves with institutions larger than their needs are making sections available to Catholic charities, for lay retreats and Cursillos, and for Head Start and Upward Bound programs.

There is a growing concern among many that the really poor do not receive the attention they deserve, and thought and effort are being given to the correction of this lack, both by education of the poor themselves and by specialized

education of those who will be in contact with them. Recently I heard the possibility of a mobile school for migrant
workers' children being discussed, a convent on wheels
which would move with the workers, teaching the children
where they were when they were free. The practical problem of state certification, with each state having its own
requirements and standards, was brushed aside by the young
woman who had conceived the dream. "They aren't getting
any education at the present time," she said dryly. "Why
should anyone quibble about certification?" This combina-
tion convent and ungraded school on wheels might be sub-
sidized either by the congregation staffing it or through the
federal government's funds for the underprivileged. It would
require only a small faculty, but a specially trained, dedicated one, eager and able to awaken in this deprived group
of our citizenry an eagerness to "grow in its ability to
wonder, to understand, to contemplate, to make personal
judgments, and to develop a religious, moral, and social
sense," [11] as well as in the basic intellectual competencies
demanded of the literate man in the twentieth century in
order to liberate him from the miseries of ignorance. The
Council took special note of this need when it stated that,
"because of illiteracy and a lack of responsible activity,
man will be prevented from collaborating in a truly human
manner for the sake of the common good." [12]

Greater social awareness is evidenced in projects such as
the Notre Dame Sisters' Urban Training Center at St. Ambrose, Chicago. Members will teach part-time in a poverty-
funded education project, an inner-city remedial and en-
richment school. In addition to learning firsthand techniques
of adapting curriculum and methods to minority-group
children, the teachers will audit in and be apprenticed to
such community agencies as self-help programs, girls' juven-
ile court, Illinois Council on Human Relations, Marillac
House, and Cook County Welfare Adult Training Program.[13] Mother Elred, provincial of the De Kalb province
sponsoring the project, explains the in-service training objective of the center. "Since many sisters have family back-
grounds which are principally white and middle-class, it is

not always easy for them to understand new cultures represented by our minority school children. Curriculum must be adapted; new teaching methods must be found; family customs and religious background must be understood and respected. Ford Foundation studies show that by 1970 one out of every two American children will be educationally deprived, and the fifteen major cities will be over 50 percent Negro. We must prepare to meet these educational needs. Thus, the Notre Dame Urban Training Center is an in-service teachers' leadership course in response to a grave educational problem." [14] Sisters attending the course will be prepared to give leadership to other groups which serve those suffering discrimination and deprivation.

Another experiment happily duplicated, one suspects, in many cities of the nation, was that conducted during the summer of 1967 by a group of young nuns, School Sisters of St. Francis, at St. Elizabeth's parish, Milwaukee. The nuns taught sewing of children's clothing to inner-core mothers, some of them, undoubtedly, mothers of the Head Start youngsters who were in classrooms on the first floor being taught by the Sisters of Notre Dame. The purpose of the Center was threefold, "to help the people in the inner core to realize the Church is interested in them, to help the sisters realize the needs there, and to teach some of the residents to help themselves by sewing for their children." A positive approach, like the Head Start program, it is open to all interested, Catholic or not.[15]

The National Catholic Conference for Interracial Justice, in addition to its teams of Traveling Workshops, inaugurated a college teacher exchange during the summer of 1967. Approximately twenty nuns from northern colleges with masters and doctorates taught courses in their academic fields on fifteen Southern campuses. The services freed Southern instructors for further summer education and gave the visiting professors experiences which would enrich their own lives and their students enrolled in courses on the home campuses.[16]

Obviously, nuns are concerned in adapting their work to the needs of today. Aware of their responsibilities as individuals, they are equally convinced that their single contribution gains strength through group effort, and that the involvement of the community in their separate activities insures both stability and growth. Like Father Pedro Arrupe, superior general of the Jesuits, they are very much aware of the danger in repeating yesterday's answers to tomorrow's problems, of talking in a way men no longer understand, of speaking a language which does not speak to the heart of living men. They are engaged in preparing their young members for the world of tomorrow while attempting to adjust to the needs of today.

This book has not dealt with one of the more popular subjects of discussion, the religious habit, chiefly because it has been dealt with at such length, with arguments pro and con filling balanced columns in many periodicals and diocesan newspapers, and also while relatively insignificant, it is a subject each congregation is working on individually. Some, it is true, seem to have been content with minor changes not visible to any but the initiate, while others have opted for the adoption of a completely secular garb, suit, or dress. Some wear hats, some veils; some retain the long skirt, some have shortened it; and some are still debating. Some have chosen to match the habit to the assignment of the individual sister, and if one can venture a guess on anything so unpredictable as a universal feminine decision in the matter of dress, I would suspect that it is this latter adjustment which will be most frequently seen in the future. The nun may wear a different habit for the various apostolic situations in which she finds herself, retaining the standard habit of the congregation when it is feasible, adapting it when necessity requires. The Council itself made no specific suggestions other than to note that "since they are signs of a consecrated life, religious habits should be simple and modest, at once poor and becoming. They should meet the requirements of health, and be suited to the circumstances of time and place as well as to the services required by those who wear them." [17]

That the religious habit should be dropped completely seems not to be indicated by the emphasis on its sign value

in the document, and by Pope Paul VI when he spoke on
March 7, 1967, to the major superiors gathered for the
International Union of Superiors General of Religious Orders of Women. Said the Pope: "Modifications are undoubtedly necessary, yet care should be taken that the
religious habit, by its simplicity and its modesty, always
remains, according to the long tradition of the Church and
the wise prescription of the conciliar decree, a *signum con-
secrationis,* that is, a visible sign, recognizable by all, of the
state of life embraced by the consecrated virgin." [18]

The standard for renewal in this, as in the entire area
of religious life, was beautifully summarized by Sister Jerome
Marie, ssND. She tells of an incident which occurred in the
fall of 1960 when the Kennedy-Nixon campaign was blazing
to a close. Sister was standing in the lobby of a public
library, glancing over an array of books, when a woman
with a pre-school child came in the door. The little girl
broke away from her mother's grasp and ran over to Sister,
her shoes resounding on the marble floor. But let Sister
Jerome Marie tell it:

"Hi, nun," she said.

"Hi," I returned.

"She looked at me for another instant, and then said, 'I
know who you're for.' Through my mind flashed the thought
that this precocious child had overheard the political con-
versations of her parents, but before the idea could crystal-
lize, she finished her statement. 'You're for God.'

"I have thought many times of her implicit, unerring sum-
mation of my reason for being what I am. Perhaps this
child has stated the answer to some current problems in
religious life.

"Shall we wear black and white, or 'living color'? Long
skirts or short skirts? Forehead bands or silvered strands? The
one consideration which supersedes all others is this: will
this garb show the world that we're for God? Not that we're
up-to-date; not that we're chic; not that we're practical; not
that we're at ease in any social situation; but that we are
God's. This standard doesn't exclude the others, but it
doesn't automatically include them, either. All the others

must harmonize with it. What shall we wear? . . . What best tells others that we're for God?" [19]

This then, is not only the reason behind the habit, traditional or radically changed; it is also the reason for the nun. It was the reason behind Mary's *fiat,* as it is the reason why her daughters through the centuries have imitated her in total giving, and why, whatever they wear or whatever the externals of their lives, there will always be religious. After the tragic fire at Our Lady of Angels school in Chicago, a reporter, editorializing on the deaths of the sisters, wrote, "Their holocaust was not in the line of duty; it was the burning tribute of their love." He was right, of course, for the taking of vows has as its object a reaching to Christ interiorly in the deepening of the baptismal commitment, and a reaching out to him in others apostolically. In both it is the same Christ.

That is perhaps why it is so difficult to explain what is happening in religious life. There is a great ferment, a very real attempt to discover what the needs of an evolving world really are in order to meet them. Mistakes are being made as new approaches are being tried, in some cases experiments bypassed because there is not time for experimentation. And there have been magnificent examples of success in works. But through all the obvious changes, the new and exciting ideas about the Church, the mystery of God's love that selects some souls to serve him in this specific way remains. Any attempt to explain it with human language continues to be futile; all that can be done with words is to describe the works, and perhaps that is all that is necessary, for by their works you shall know them.

Appendix A

Decree on the Appropriate Renewal of the Religious Life

(*Perfectae Caritatis*)

PAUL, BISHOP
SERVANT OF THE SERVANTS OF GOD
TOGETHER WITH THE FATHERS OF THE SACRED COUNCIL
FOR EVERLASTING MEMORY

1. In its Constitution which begins, "The Light of the World," [2] this most sacred Synod has already pointed out how the teaching and example of the Divine Master laid the foundation for a pursuit of perfect charity [3] through the exercise of the evangelical counsels, [4] and how such a pursuit serves as a blazing emblem of the heavenly kingdom. In this present document, the Synod intends to deal with the life and rules of those institutes whose members profess chastity, poverty, and obedience, and to make provisions for their needs as the tenor of the times indicates. [5]

From the very infancy of the Church, there have existed men and women who strove to follow Christ more freely and

1. *De accommodata renovatione*, often translated "on the adaptation and renewal." The Decree will clarify the two points involved. See, for example, Art. 2.
2. The Dogmatic Constitution on the Church, promulgated Nov. 21, 1964. Ch. 6 of that Constitution should be read first by anyone studying this Decree.
3. In the official Latin, the Decree begins with this phrase: *Perfectae caritatis* ("perfect charity," "complete love"), a very appropriate opening. See Art. 15 for extended treatment of the topic.
4. Evangelical counsels: these have been traditionally associated with poverty, chastity, and obedience, as the concrete realization of our Lord's invitation found in the Gospel according to St. Matthew (19:21; 19:10-12). Cf. Constitution on the Church, Art. 43.
5. *Prout tempora nostra suadent*. The Decree here touches on the theme of updating or modernization, which will recur throughout the document. See especially the beginning of Art. 2 and its section d.

imitate Him more nearly by the practice of the evangelical counsels. Each in his own way, these souls have led a life dedicated to God. Under the influence of the Holy Spirit, many of them pursued a solitary life,[6] or founded religious families to which the Church willingly gave the welcome and approval of her authority.

And so it happened by divine plan that a wonderful variety of religious communities grew up. This variety contributed mightily toward making the Church experienced in every good deed (cf. 2 Tim. 3:17 and ready for a ministry of service [7] in building up Christ's body (cf. Eph. 4:12). Not only this, but adorned by the various gifts of her children, the Church became radiant like a bride made beautiful for her spouse (cf. Apoc. 21:2); and through her God's manifold wisdom could reveal itself (cf. Eph. 3:10).

But whatever the diversity of their spiritual endowments, all who are called by God to practice the evangelical counsels, and who do so faithfully, devote themselves in a special way to the Lord. They imitate Christ the virgin and the poor man (cf. Mt. 8:20; Lk. 9:58), who, by an obedience which carried Him even to death on the cross (cf. Phil. 2:8), redeemed men and made them holy. As a consequence, impelled by a love which the Holy Spirit has poured into their hearts (cf. Rom. 5:5), these Christians spend themselves ever increasingly for Christ, and for His body the Church (cf. Col. 1:24).

Hence the more ardently they unite themselves to Christ through a self-surrender involving their entire lives, the more vigorous becomes the life of the Church and the more abundantly her apostolate bears fruit.

A life consecrated by a profession of the counsels is of surpassing value. Such a life has a necessary role to play in the circumstances of the present age. That this kind of life and its contemporary role may achieve greater good for the Church, this sacred Synod issues the following decrees. They concern only the general principles which must underlie an

6. The reference is to those who lived as hermits.
7. A constant theme of the Second Vatican Council, and a basic theme of Christianity.

appropriate renewal of the life and rules of religious communities. These principles apply also to societies living a community life without the exercise of vows,[8] and to secular institutes,[9] though the special character of both groups is to be maintained. After the Council, the competent authority will be obliged to enact particular laws opportunely spelling out and apply what is legislated here.

2. The appropriate renewal [10] of religious life involves two simultaneous processes: (1) a continuous return to the sources of all Christian life and to the original inspiration behind a given community [11] and (2) an adjustment of the community to the changed conditions of the times. It is according to the following principles that such renewal should go forward under the influence of the Holy Spirit and the guidance of the Church.

a) Since the fundamental norm of the religious life is a following of Christ as proposed by the gospel, such is to be regarded by all communities as their supreme law.

b) It serves the best interests of the Church for communities to have their own special character and purpose. Therefore loyal recognition and safekeeping should be accorded to the spirit of founders, as also to all the particular goals and wholesome traditions which constitute the heritage of each community.

---

8. These organizations (e.g., Sulpicians, Maryknollers) are often called "societies of common life."

9. Secular institutes are associations of priests or laity or both. Their members live the life of the vows or promises of poverty, chastity and obedience without the protections of religious habit, cloistered room, or spiritual exercises in common. Secular institutes differ from Third Order groups, Sodalities, and Catholic Action organizations because the institutes involve profession of poverty, chastity, and obedience and have been given a special place in the canonical structure of the Church.

10. As indicated by Pope John in originally summoning the Council, this renewal was primarily a "New Pentecost." The "fresh air" he longed to see within the Church was chiefly the breath of the Holy Spirit in renewal.

11. "Institutes" is a more literal translation of the word used in the Latin text here. "Community" is widely used by religious congregations to mean what the technical word 'institute" stands for, i.e., a whole order, society, or congregation (as is clear from Art. 13, speaking of "provinces and houses of a religious community").—Ed.

c) All communities should participate in the life of the Church. According to its individual character, each should make its own and foster in every possible way the enterprises and objectives of the Church in such fields as these: the scriptural, liturgical, doctrinal, pastoral, ecumenical, missionary, and social.

d) Communities should promote among their members a suitable awareness of contemporary human conditions and of the needs of the Church. For if their members can combine the burning zeal of an apostle with wise judgments, made in the light of faith, concerning the circumstances of the modern world, they will be able to come to the aid of men more effectively.

e) Since the religious life is intended above all else to lead those who embrace it to an imitation of Christ and to union with God through the profession of the evangelical counsels, the fact must be honestly faced that even the most desirable changes made on behalf of contemporary needs will fail of their purpose unless a renewal of spirit gives life to them.[12] Indeed such an interior renewal must always be accorded the leading role even in the promotion of exterior works.

3. The manner of living, praying, and working should be suitably adapted to the physical and psychological conditions of todays religious and also, to the extent required by the nature of each community, to the needs of the apostolate, the requirements of a given culture,[13] the social and economic circumstances anywhere, but especially in missionary territories.

The way in which communities are governed should also be re-examined in the light of these same standards.

For this reason constitutions, directories, custom books,[14] books of prayers and ceremonies, and similar compilations are to be suitably revised and brought into harmony with

12. A Key sentence of the Decree, and, in fact, a key principle of the whole spiritual life.
13. Adaptation of the religious life to the local culture is vital, especially in missionary work. The failure of some missionary activity is due precisely to neglect of this adaptation.
14. Custom books are handbooks of observances approved in a province or region of a religious order.

the documents of this sacred Synod. This task will require the suppression of outmoded regulations.

4. Successful renewal and proper adaptation cannot be achieved unless every member of a community cooperates.[15]

In the work of appropriate renewal, it is the responsibility of competent authorities alone, especially of general chapters,[16] to issue norms, to pass laws, and to allow for a right amount of prudent experimentation, though in all such matters, according to the norm of law, the approval of the Holy See and of local Ordinaries must be given when it is required. In decisions which involve the future of an institute as a whole, superiors should in appropriate manner consult the members and give them a hearing.

For the suitable renewal of convents of nuns, their wishes and recommendations can also be ascertained from meetings of federations or from other assemblies lawfully convoked.

Let all bear in mind, however, that the hope of renewal must be lodged in a more diligent observance of rule and of constitution rather than in a multiplication of individual laws.

5. The members of each community should recall above everything else that by their profession of the evangelical counsels they have given answer to a divine call to live for God alone not only by dying to sin (cf. Rom. 6:11) but also by renouncing the world. They have handed over their entire lives to God's service in an act of special consecration which is deeply rooted in their baptismal consecration and which provides an ampler manifestation of it.

Inasmuch as their self-dedication has been accepted by the Church, they should realize that they are committed to her service as well.

15. Art. 4 touches on the proper relationship between authorities and members in religious communities. Note that the Decree, consistent with the Council's teaching on authority as a role of service, does not call religious men and women 'subjects" but *sodales,* i.e., fellow members. There is much more on the topic in Art. 14.

16. In the spirit of the Decree, a number of religious orders (e.g., Jesuits, Franciscans) even before the end of the Council announced plans for the meeting of their general chapter or congregation to work out appropriate renewal for their communities.

The fact that they are in God's service should ignite and fan within them the exercise of virtues, especially humility, obedience, courage, and chastity. Through them they share spiritually in Christ's self-surrender (cf. Phil. 2:7-8) and in His life (cf. Rom. 8:1-13).

Therefore, in fidelity to their profession and in renunciation of all things for the sake of Christ (cf. Mk. 10:28), let religious follow Him (cf. Mt. 19:21) as their one necessity (cf. Lk. 10:42). Let them listen to His words (cf. Lk. 10:39) and be preoccupied with His work (cf. 1 Cor. 7:32).

To this end, as they seek God before all things and only Him, the members of each community should combine contemplation with apostolic love. By the former they adhere to God in mind and heart; by the latter they strive to associate themselves with the work of redemption and to spread the Kingdom of God.

6. Those who profess the evangelical counsels love and seek before all else that God who took the initiative in loving us (cf. 1 Jn. 4:10); in every circumstance they aim to develop a life hidden with Christ in God (cf. Col. 3:3). Such dedication gives rise and urgency to the love of one's neighbor for the world's salvation and the upbuilding of the Church. From this love the very practice of the evangelical counsels takes life and direction.

Therefore, drawing on the authentic sources of Christian spirituality, let the members of communities energetically cultivate the spirit of prayer and the practice of it. In the first place they should take the sacred Scriptures in hand each day by way of attaining "the excelling knowledge of Jesus Christ" (Phil. 3:8) through reading these divine writings and meditating on them. They should enact the sacred liturgy, especially the most holy mystery of the Eucharist, with hearts and voices attuned to the Church; here is a most copious source of nourishment for the spiritual life.

Fed thus at the table of the divine law and of the sacred altar, they can bring a brother's love to the members of Christ, and a son's love to their revered pastors; thus they can live and think with the Church [17] to an ever-increasing degree, and spend themselves completely on her mission.

7. Members of those communities which are totally dedicated to contemplation give themselves to God alone in solitude and silence and through constant prayer and ready penance.[18] No matter how urgent may be the needs of the active apostolate, such communities will always have a distinguished part to play in Christ's Mystical Body, where "all members have not the same function" (Rom. 12:4). For they offer God a choice sacrifice of praise. They brighten God's people with the richest splendors of sanctity. By their example they motivate this people; by imparting a hidden, apostolic fruitfulness, they make this people grow. Thus they are the glory of the Church and an overflowing fountain of heavenly graces. Nevertheless, their manner of living should be revised according to the aforementioned principles and standards of appropriate renewal, though their withdrawal from the world and the practices of their contemplative life should be maintained at their holiest.

8. There exist within the Church a great number of clerical and lay institutes devoted to various aspects of the apostolate.[19] They have contributions to make which are as various as the graces given them: some exercise a ministry of service, some teach doctrine, some encourage through exhortation, some give in simplicity, or bring cheerfulness to the sorrowful [20] (cf. Rom. 12:5-8). "Now there are varieties of gifts, but the same Spirit" (1 Cor. 12:4).

In such communities the very nature of the religious life requires apostolic action and services, since a sacred ministry and a special work of charity have been consigned to them

17. The phrase "think with the Church" will recall to many readers the "Rules for Thinking with the Church" at the end of St. Ignatius Loyola's Spiritual Exercises. The Council expresses the idea in connection with the Bible and the liturgy (at the beginning of the sentence).
18. E.g., Carthusians, Cistercians (Trappists), Carmelites of the Strict Observance.
19. The reference is to orders, congregations and societies of priests, brothers and sisters engaged in a wide variety of work: parishes, schools, retreats, etc.
20. *Qui miseretur in hilaritate:* almost inevitably one thinks of St. Philip Neri, the "jolly" saint, and of Pope John XXIII.

by the Church and must be discharged in her name. Hence the entire religious life of the members of these communities should be penetrated by an apostolic spirit, as their entire apostolic activity should be animated by a religious spirit.[21] Therefore, in order that members may above all respond to their vocation of following Christ and may serve Christ Himself in His members, their apostolic activity should result from an intimate union with Him. In this way it will happen that love for God and neighbor will itself be nurtured.

These communities, then, should skillfully harmonize their observances and practices with the needs of the apostolate to which they are dedicated. But inasmuch as the religious life which is committed to apostolic works takes on many forms, a necessary diversity will have to distinguish its path to a suitable renewal, and members of the various communities will have to be sustained in living for Christ's service by means which are proper and fitting for themselves.

9. In the East and in the West, the venerable institution of monastic life should be faithfully preserved, and should grow ever-increasingly radiant with its own authentic spirit. Through the long course of the centuries, this institution has proved its merits splendidly to the Church and to human society.[22] The main task of monks is to render to the Divine Majesty a service at once simple and noble, within the monastic confines. This they do either by devoting themselves entirely to divine worship in a life that is hidden, or by lawfully taking up some apostolate or works of Christian charity. While safeguarding the proper identity of each institution, let monasteries be renewed in their ancient and beneficial traditions, and so adapt them to the modern needs of souls that monasteries will be seedbeds of growth [23] for the Christian people.

There are religious communities which by rule or constitution closely join the apostolic life with choral prayer and mo-

21. Again the interpenetration of action and contemplation.
22. The following sentences of the Decree give a description of the monastic life (as found, for example, in the Benedictine Order).
23. *Seminaria sint aedificationis*, "institutions of edification," in the terminology of many classical works on the subject.

nastic observances.[24] Let these groups, too, so harmonize their manner of life with the requirements of the apostolate belonging to them that they still faithfully preserve their form of life, for it is one which serves the highest welfare of the Church.

10. The lay religious life, for both men and women, constitutes a state which of itself is one of total dedication to the profession of the evangelical counsels.[25] This sacred Synod highly esteems such a ·life, since it serves the pastoral work of the Church so usefully by educating the young, caring for the sick, and discharging other services. The Council supports such religious in their vocation, and entreats them to adapt their life to modern needs.

This sacred Synod declares that there is no objection to religious congregations of brothers admitting some members to holy orders, to supply needed priestly ministrations for their own houses, provided that the lay character of the congregation remains unchanged and that it is the general chapter that makes the decision.

11. Secular institutes are not religious communities but they carry with them in the world a profession of the evangelical counsels which is genuine and complete, and recognized as such by the Church.[26] This profession confers a consecration on men and women, laity and clergy, who reside in the world. For this reason they should chiefly strive for total self-dedication to God, one inspired by perfect charity. These institutes should preserve their proper and particular character, a secular one, so that they may everywhere measure up

24. Many Catholic girls and women are familiar with this type of community in the Religious of the Society of the Sacred Heart and other dedicated women who conduct academies and colleges around the world.

25. The Council warmly commends the work of religious brothers and sisters.

26. Secular institutes differ from religious institutes in this: their profession of poverty, chastity, and obedience is by some act other than *public* vows, and community of life is not required. This form of the life of evangelical perfection in the world was first given official recognition by the Holy See in the constitution *Provida Mater* (Feb. 2, 1947). The secular institute form of life should not be confused with either the religious life or lay apostolates such as Catholic Action.

successfully to that apostolate which they were designed
to exercise, and which is both in the world and, in a sense,
of the world.[27]

Yet they should surely realize that they cannot acquit
themselves of so immense a task unless their members are
skillfully trained in matters both human and divine, and can
thus be a genuine leaven in the world for strengthening
and enlarging Christ's body. Therefore directors should give
especially serious care to the spiritual training of members
and to the promotion of more advanced formation as well.

12. That chastity which is practiced "on behalf of the
heavenly Kingdom" (Mt. 19:12), and which religious profess, deserves to be esteemed as a surpassing gift of grace.
For it liberates the human heart in a unique way (cf. 1
Cor. 7:32-35) and causes it to burn with greater love for
God and all mankind. It is therefore an outstanding token
of heavenly riches, and also a most suitable way for religious to spend themselves readily in God's service and in
works of the apostolate. Religious thereby give witness to all
Christ's faithful of that wondrous marriage between the
Church and Christ her only spouse, a union which has been
established by God and will be fully manifested in the world
to come.

Hence, as they strive to live their profession faithfully, religious do well to lodge their faith in the words of the Lord;
trusting in God's help rather than presuming on their own
resources, let them practice mortification and custody of the
senses. They should take advantage of those natural helps
which favor mental and bodily health. As a result they will
not be influenced by those erroneous claims [28] which present
complete continence as impossible or as harmful to human
development. In addition a certain spiritual instinct should

27. *In saeculo ac veluti ex saeculo.* The word "secular" in the term
"secular institute" is based on the Latin word for "world"; as the
Decree itself here stresses, that word properly distinguishes these institutes from others.
28. This is the nearest the Decree comes to language of condemnation.
The Council here confronts a recurring objection made by some people
in the world. Firmly (but also gently, in the spirit of Pope John)
the Council takes a stand.

lead them to spurn everything likely to imperil chastity. Above all, everyone should remember—superiors especially —that chastity has stronger safeguards in a community when true fraternal love thrives among its members.[29]

Since the observance of total continence intimately involves the deeper inclinations of human nature, candidates should not undertake the profession of chastity nor be admitted to its profession except after a truly adequate testing period [30] and only if they have the needed degree of psychological and emotional maturity. They should not only be warned of the dangers confronting chastity, but be trained to make a celibate life consecrated to God part of the richness of their whole personality.

13. Poverty voluntarily embraced in imitation of Christ provides a witness which is highly esteemed, especially today.[31] Let religious painstakingly cultivate such poverty, and give it new expressions if need be. By it a man shares in the poverty of Christ, who became poor for our sake when before He had been rich, that we might be enriched by His poverty (cf. 2 Cor. 8:9; Mt. 8:20).

Religious poverty requires more than limiting the use of possessions to the consent of superiors; members of a community ought to be poor in both fact and spirit, and have their treasures in heaven (cf. Mt. 6:20).

In discharging his duty, each religious should regard himself as subject to the common law of labor. While making necessary provisions for their livelihood and undertakings, religious should brush aside all undue concern and entrust themselves to the providence of the heavenly Father (cf. Mt. 6:25).

29. The sentence expresses a valuable insight. See the end of the next paragraph for another important insight.
30. This testing period usually has two parts, postulancy (a short initial period) and noviceship (one or two years induration). At the end of noviceship (novitiate), the promises or vows are pronounced. During the noviceship period the candidate examines the life of the institute and superiors examine the candidate (to judge, among other things, the psychological and emotional maturity to which the Decree refers here).
31. I.e., by those (the Council Fathers, et al.) who understand what has been handed down from sacred Scripture on the subject.

In their constitutions, religious communities can allow their members to renounce any inheritance which they have acquired or are due to acquire.[32]

Depending on the circumstances of their location, communities as such should aim at giving a kind of corporate witness to their own poverty. Let them willingly contribute something from their own resources to the other needs of the Church, and to the support of the poor, whom religious should love with the tenderness of Christ (cf. Mt. 19:21; 25:34-46; Jas. 2:15-16; 1 Jn. 3:17). Provinces and houses of a religious community should share their resources with one another, those which are better supplied assisting those which suffer need.

To the degree that their rules and constitutions permit, religious communities can rightly possess whatever is necessary for their temporal life and their mission. Still, let them avoid every appearance of luxury, of excessive wealth, and accumulation of possessions.

14. Through the profession of obedience, religious offer to God a total dedication of their own wills as a sacrifice of themselves; they thereby unite themselves with greater steadiness and security to the saving will of God. In this way they follow the pattern of Jesus Christ, who came to do the Father's will (cf. Jn. 4:34; 5:30; Heb. 10:7; Ps. 39:9). "Taking the nature of a slave" (Phil. 2:7), He learned obedience from His sufferings (cf. Heb. 5:8). Under the influence of the Holy Spirit, religious submit themselves to their superiors, whom faith presents as God's representatives, and through whom they are guided into the service of all their brothers in Christ. Thus did Christ Himself out of submission to the Father minister to the brethren and surrender His life as a ransom for many (cf. Mt. 20:28; Jn. 10:14-18). In this way, too, religious assume a firmer commitment to the ministry of the Church and labor to achieve the mature measure of the fullness of Christ (cf. Eph. 4:13).

32. Until promulgation of this Decree, renunciation of inheritance had been a distinguishing mark of final and solemn vows as distinguished from temporary and simple vows.

Therefore, in a spirit of faith and of love for God's will, let religious show humble obedience to their superiors in accord with the norms of rule and constitution. Realizing that they are giving service to the upbuilding of Christ's body according to God's design, let them bring to the execution of commands and to the discharge of assignments entrusted to them the resources of their minds and wills, and their gifts of nature and grace. Lived in this manner, religious obedience will not diminish the dignity of the human person but will rather lead it to maturity in consequence of that enlarged freedom which belongs to the sons of God.

For his part, as one who will render an account for the souls entrusted to him (cf. Heb. 13:17), each superior should himself be docile to God's will in the exercise of his office. Let him use his authority in a spirit of service for the brethren, and manifest thereby [33] the charity with which God loves them. Governing his subjects as God's own sons, and with regard for their human personality, a superior will make it easier for them to obey gladly. Therefore he must make a special point of leaving them appropriately free with respect to the sacrament of penance and direction of conscience. Let him give the kind of leadership which will encourage religious to bring an active and responsible obedience to the offices they shoulder and the activities they undertake. Therefore a superior should listen willingly to his subjects and encourage them to make a personal contribution to the welfare of the community and of the Church. Not to be weakened, however, is the superior's authority to decide what must be done and to require the doing of it.

Let chapters [34] and councils faithfully acquit themselves of the governing role given to them; each should express in its own way the fact that all members of the community have a share in the welfare of the whole community and a responsibility for it.

33. In the following phrase the Decree touches on one of the profound theological truths that lie behind the theme of service.
34. Some religious orders have other terms to denote these bodies of delegates who legislate for the whole community or institute (e.g., the Jesuits have a General Congregation).

15. The primitive Church provided an example of community life when the multitude of believers were of one heart and one mind (cf. Acts 4:32), and found nourishment in the teaching of the gospel and in the sacred liturgy, especially the Eucharist. Let such a life continue in prayerfulness and a sharing of the same spirit (cf. Acts 2:42). As Christ's members living fraternally together, let them excel one another in showing respect (cf. Rom. 12:10), and let each carry the other's burdens (cf. Gal. 6:2). For thanks to God's love poured into hearts by the Holy Spirit (cf. Rom. 5:5), a religious community is a true family gathered together in the Lord's name and rejoicing in His presence (cf. Mt. 18:20). For love is the fulfillment of the law (cf. Rom. 13:10) and the bond of perfection (cf. Col. 3:14); where it exists we know we have been taken from death to life (cf. 1 Jn. 3:14). In fact, brotherly unity shows that Christ has come (cf. Jn. 13:35; 17:21); from it results great apostolic influence.

To strengthen the bond of brotherhood between members of a community, those who are called lay brothers, assistants, or some other name,[35] should be brought into the heart of its life and activities. Unless the state of affairs suggests otherwise, care must be taken to produce in women's communities a single category of sister. Then there may be retained only such distinction between persons as is demanded by the diversity of the works for which sisters are destined by a special call from God or by particular aptitude.

According to the norms of their constitutions, monasteries and communities of men which are not exclusively lay in their character can admit both clergy and laity on the same basis and with equal rights and duties, excepting those which result from ordination.

16. The papal cloister [36] for nuns totally dedicated to contemplation is to be retained. Still, it should be modified according to the conditions of time and place, and outdated

35. E.g., coadjutor brothers.
36. Cloister, I.e., the fact and rules of enclosure (known to monastery and convent visitors chiefly as designation of an area they may not enter) are regulated by the Holy See for the nuns referred to here (Carmelites, Poor Clares, etc.)

customs done away with. In such matters, consideration should be given to the wishes of the monasteries themselves.

Other nuns institutionally devoted to external works of the apostolate should be exempt from papal cloister so that they can better discharge the apostolic tasks assigned to them. They should, however, maintain the kind of cloister required by their constitutions.

17. Since they are signs of a consecrated life, religious habits [37] should be simple and modest, at once poor and becoming. They should meet the requirements of health and be suited to the circumstances of time and place as well as to the services required by those who wear them. Habits of men and women which do not correspond to those norms are to be changed.

18. The suitable renewal of religious communities depends very largely on the training of their members. Therefore religious men other than clerics, and religious women as well, should not be assigned to apostolic works immediately after the novitiate. In suitable residences and in a fitting manner, let them continue their training in the religious life and the apostolate, in doctrine and technical matters, even to the extent of winning appropriate degrees. [38]

Lest the adaptations of religious life to the needs of our time be merely superficial, and lest those who by constitution pursue the external apostolate prove unequal to the fulfillment of their task, religious should be properly instructed, according to the intellectual gifts and personal endowments of each, in the prevailing manners of contemporary social life, and in its characteristic ways of feeling and thinking. If such training is harmoniously coordinated it will contribute to integrity of life on the part of religious.

Throughout their lives religious should labor earnestly to perfect their spiritual, doctrinal, and professional development. As far as possible, superiors should provide them with the opportunity, the resources, and the time to do so.

It also devolves upon superiors to see that the best persons

37. Habits, i.e., the garb of religious priets, brothers, and sisters.
38. *Titulis,* educational degrees or other certificates and titles (e.g., apprentice) that are relevant to the work of religious men and women.

are chosen for directors, spiritual guides, and professors, and that they are carefully trained.

19. When there is a question of establishing new communities,[39] serious thought must be given to the need for them, or at least to their eminent usefulness, and also to the likelihood that they will prosper. Otherwise, lack of caution will give rise to communities which serve no purpose or are deprived of sufficient vitality.

Where the Church has newly taken root, special attention should be given to the establishment and development of fresh forms of religious life. These should take into account the natural endowments and the manners of the people, and also local customs and circumstances.

20. Communities should faithfully maintain and fulfill their proper activities. Yet, they should make adjustments in them according to the needs of time and place and in favor of what will benefit the universal Church and individual dioceses.[40] To this end they should resort to suitable techniques, including modern ones,[41] and abandon whatever activities are today less in keeping with the spirit of the community and its authentic character.

The missionary spirit should be thoroughly [42] maintained in religious communities, and, according to the character of each one, given a modern expression. In this way the preaching of the gospel among all peoples can be done more successfully.

21. If after consulting the appropriate Ordinaries, the Holy See decides that certain communities or monasteries no longer offer any reasonable hope of flourishing, these should be forbidden thereafter to accept novices. If it can be done, they should be absorbed by a more vigorous community or

39. New communities: not new houses or schools but new institutes, congregations, or societies. As the next paragraph shows, the Council here takes a long forward look into the future.
40. The apostolate of religious carried out in particular dioceses is also the proper concern of the local bishop. Therefore, in these adaptations it would be proper for religious to consult the bishops for advice as to what may be to the best interest of the local church.
41. *Etiam novis mediis:* perhaps "even though modern."—Sd.
42. *Omnino,* often translated "by all means."—Ed.

monastery which approximates their own purpose and spirit.

22. Where opportunity and the Holy See permit, independent communities and monasteries should work towards making a federation of themselves if they belong in some sense to the same religious family; or, if their constitutions and customs are practically the same and a kindred spirit animates them, they should try to form a union, especially when of themselves they are excessively small; or let them enter into an association if they engage in external activities of an identical or similar nature.

23. Favor is to be shown to conferences or councils of major superiors [43] which have been established by the Holy See. These can make splendid contributions to several goals: helping individual communities fulfill their purpose more adequately; fostering more successful cooperation on behalf of the Church; distributing workers in a given territory more advantageously; and working on affairs of common concern to religious communities.

Where the exercise of the apostolate is involved, appropriate coordination and collaboration with episcopal conferences should be established.

Similar conferences can also be set up for secular institutes.

24. Priests and Catholic teachers should make serious efforts [44] on behalf of religious vocations, so that a new supply may be at hand for meeting the Church's needs adequately.[45] Candidates should be appropriately and carefully selected. Ordinary sermons should treat more often of

43. Participation in such conferences or councils, especially in the case of smaller religious groups of men or women, serves to widen the apostolic horizons of particular religious institutes and can be a useful line of communication with the regional conferences of bishops.
44. Orders of priests, brothers, and sisters have rightly established the office of vocation director, vocation recruiter, etc.
45. The first task of the vocation director is to *discover* the invitation of the Holy Spirit. The director will often meet candidates who are directed by the Holy Spirit to serve in the diocesan clergy in some congregation other than his own. In such a case it will be his function to encourage such a candidate to follow this invitation—an attitude that will promote the ultimate well-being of his own institute and the entire Church.

the evangelical counsels and the choice of the religious state.
Parents should develop and protect religious vocations in
the hearts of their children by training them to behave like
Christians.

Communities have the right to spread knowledge of themselves by way of attracting vocations, and to seek out candidates as well. Only, they should do so with proper prudence,
adhering to the norms set down by the Holy See and the
local bishop.

Religious should not forget that the good example of their
own lives affords the highest recommendation for their community, and the most appealing invitation to embrace the
religious life.

25. The communities for which these norms of appropriate
renewal are decreed should react with a willing spirit to
their divine calling and their contemporary mission in the
Church. This sacred Synod has high regard for the character
of their life—virginal, poor, and obedient—of which Christ
the Lord Himself is the model. The Council places steady
hope in the immense fruitfulness of their labors, both the
unseen ones and the obvious.

Let all religious therefore spread throughout the whole
world the good news of Christ by the integrity of their faith,
their love for God and neighbor, their devotion to the Cross,
and their hope of future glory. Thus will their witness be
seen by all, and our Father in heaven will be glorified (cf.
Mt. 5:16). Thus, too, with the prayerful aid of that most
loving Virgin Mary, God's Mother, "whose life is a rule of
life for all," [46] religious communities will experience a daily
growth in numbers, and will yield a richer harvest of fruits
that bring salvation.

Each and every one of the things set forth in this Decree
has won the consent of the Fathers of this most sacred Council. We, too, by the apostolic authority conferred on us by
Christ, join with the Venerable Fathers in approving, decree-
ing, and establishing these things in the Holy Spirit, and we

46. St. Ambrose. "De Virginitate," 1, II, c. n. 15. (This is the only
non-biblical reference in the Decree.—Ed.

direct that what has thus been enacted in synod be published to God's glory.

Rome, at St. Peter's, October 28, 1965*

I, Paul, Bishop of the Catholic Church

There follow the signatures of the Fathers.

---

*Following the Decree there is an announcement entitled "A Suspension of Law" (*Vacatio legis*): "With respect to the new laws contained in this promulgated Decree, the Most Holy Father grants a suspension until June 29, 1966, that is, until the feast of Sts. Peter and Paul next year. In the meantime the Supreme Pontiff will issue norms for the implementation of the aforementioned laws. Rome, October 28, 1965. ✠ Pericle Felici, Titular Archbishop of Samosata, Secretary General of the Most Holy Council."—Ed.

Appendix B

Dogmatic Constitution on the Church

(*Lumen Gentium*)

PAUL, BISHOP
SERVANT OF THE SERVANTS OF GOD
TOGETHER WITH THE FATHERS OF THE SACRED COUNCIL
FOR EVERLASTING MEMORY

CHAPTER VI

RELIGIOUS [207]

43. The evangelical counsels of chastity dedicated to God, poverty, and obedience are based upon the words and example of the Lord.[208] They were further commended by the apostles and the Fathers, and other teachers and shepherds of the Church. The counsels are a divine gift, which the Church has received from her Lord and which she ever preserves with the help of His grace. Church authority has the

207. This chapter may be regarded as an extension of Chap. V, especially the last paragraphs. It deals with a special manner of following the universal call to holiness. The religious are not a third state in addition to the clergy and laity, but they are clerics or lay people who have dedicated themselves to a life according to the evangelical counsels, and thus differ from those pursuing the secular form of life discussed in Chap. IV. In order to indicate its special esteem for the religious life, the Council wished to devote to it a special chapter of the Constitution on the Church. Some aspects of the religious state are discussed more fully in the Decree on the Appropriate Renewal of the Religious Life.

208. In this compact paragraph, the Constitution explains in what sense the three counsels of poverty, chastity, and obedience deserve to be called "evangelical." The religious life, considered as a stable form of existence, was not directly established by Christ Himself, but it has become a permanent feature of the Church by a legitimate and necessary development. In connection with the variety of forms which the religious life has taken in the course of history, the Council distinguishes between the solitary life and life in community, pointing out some advantages of the latter.

146

duty, under the inspiration of the Holy Spirit, of interpreting these evangelical counsels, of regulating their practice, and finally of establishing stable forms of living according to them.

Thus it has come about that various forms of solitary and community life, as well as different religious families have grown up. Advancing the progress of their members and the welfare of the whole body of Christ,[209] these groups have been like branches sprouting out wondrously and abundantly from a tree growing in the field of the Lord from a seed divinely planted.

These religious families give their members the support of greater stability in their way of life, a proven method of acquiring perfection, fraternal association in the militia of Christ, and liberty strengthened by obedience. Thus these religious can securely fulfill and faithfully observe their religious profession, and rejoicing in spirit make progress on the road of charity.[210]

From the point of view of the divine and hierarchical structure of the Church, the religious state of life is not an intermediate one between the clerical and lay states. Rather, the faithful of Christ are called by God from both these latter states of life so that they may enjoy this particular gift in the life of the Church and thus each in his own way can forward the saving mission of the Church.[211]

44. The faithful of Christ can bind themselves to the three previously mentioned counsels either by vows, or by other

209. Cf. H. Rosweyde. "Vitae patrum" (Antwerp. 1628); "Apophthegmata patrum": PG 65; Palladius, "Historia lausiaca": PG 34, 995 ff. (ed. C. Butler, Cambridge, 1898 [1904]); the apostolic constitution of Pius XI, "Umbratilem," July 8, 1924: AAS 16 (1924), pp. 386-7; and Pius XII, allocution "Nous sommes heureux." Apr. 11, 1958: AAS 50 (1958). p. 283.

210. Paul VI, allocution "Magno Gaudio," May 23, 1964: AAS 56 (1964), p. 566.

211. Cf. Code of Canon Law, cc. 487 and 488, 4; PIUS XII, allocution "Annus sacer," Dec. 8, 1950: AAS 43 (1951), pp. 27 f.; and Pius XII, apostolic constitution "Provida Mater," Feb. 2, 1947: AAS 39 (1947), pp. 120 ff.

sacred bonds which are like vows in their purpose.[212] Through such a bond a person is totally dedicated to God by an act of supreme love, and is committed to the honor and service of God under a new and special title.

It is true that through baptism he has died to sin and has been consecrated to God. However, in order to derive more abundant fruit from this baptismal grace, he intends, by the profession of the evangelical counsels in the Church, to free himself from those obstacles which might draw him away from the fervor of charity and the perfection of divine worship. Thus he is more intimately consecrated to divine service.[213] This consecration gains in perfection since by virtue of firmer and steadier bonds it serves as a better symbol of the unbreakable link between Christ and His Spouse, the Church.

By the charity to which they lead,[214] the evangelical counsels join their followers to the Church and her mystery in a special way.[215] Since this is so, the spiritual life of these followers should be devoted to the welfare of the whole Church. Thence arises their duty of working to implant and strengthen the kingdom of Christ in souls and to extend that kingdom to every land. This duty is to be discharged to the extent of their capacities and in keeping with the form of their proper vocation. The chosen means may be prayer or active undertakings. It is for this reason that the Church

212. To constitute a person a "religious" in the wide sense here used, it is sufficient that he embrace an approved form of life in which he is permanently bound to live according to the three "evangelical counsels," whether the bond takes the form of vows or some other sacred commitment (such as a promise or oath). See the various categories enumerated in the Decree on the Appropriate Renewal of the Religious Life.
213. *Paul VI, as cited in footnote 210, p. 567.*
214. *Cf. St. Thomas, "Summa Theol.," 2-2, q. 184, a. 3 and q. 188 a. 2; and St. Bonaventure, Opusc. XI, "Apologia pauperum," c. 3, 3: ed. Quaracchi, t. 8, 1898, p. 245 a.*
215. This document, because its subject matter is the Church, takes occasion to stress the way in which the religious profession unites a person to the Church, thus offsetting an excessively individualistic theology of the religious life, which has sometimes prevailed in the past. The way in which the religious life contributes to the life of the Church by giving testimony to the kingdom of heaven was already mentioned earlier in Art. 31.

preserves and fosters the special character of her various religious communities.

The profession of the evangelical counsels, then, appears as a sign which can and ought to attract all the members of the Church to an effective and prompt fulfillment of the duties of their Christian vocation. The People of God has no lasting city here below, but looks forward to one which is to come. This being so, the religious state by giving its members greater freedom from earthly cares more adequately manifests to all believers the presence of heavenly goods already possessed here below.

Furthermore, it not only witnesses to the fact of a new and eternal life acquired by the redemption of Christ. It foretells the resurrected state and the glory of the heavenly kingdom. Christ also proposed to His disciples that form of life which He, as the Son of God, accepted in entering this world to do the will of the Father. In the Church this same state of life is imitated with particular accuracy and perpetually exemplified. The religious state reveals in a unique way that the kingdom of God and its overmastering necessities are superior to all earthly considerations. Finally, to all men it shows wonderfully at work within the Church the surpassing greatness of the force of Christ the King and the boundless power of the Holy Spirit.

Thus, although the religious state constituted by the profession of the evangelical counsels does not belong to the hierarchical structure of the Church, nevertheless it belongs inseparably to her life and holiness.

45. Since it is the duty of the hierarchy of the Church to nourish the People of God and lead them to the choicest pastures (cf. Ezek. 34:14), it devolves on the same hierarchy to govern with wise legislation [216] the practice of the evangelical counsels. For by that practice is uniquely fostered the perfection of love for God and neighbor.

216. *Cf. Vatican Council 1, Schema "De Ecclesia Christi," c. XV and Annotation 48: Mansi, 51, 549 f. and 619 f.; Leo XIII, epistle "Au milieu des consolations," Dec. 23, 1900; Actae Sautcae Sedis 33 (1900-1), p. 361; and Pius XII, apostolic constitution "Provida Mater," as cited in footnote 211, pp. 114 f.*

Submissively following the promptings of the Holy Spirit, the hierarchy also endorses rules formulated by eminent men and women, and authentically approves later modifications. Moreover, by its watchful and shielding authority, the hierarchy keeps close to communities established far and wide for the upbuilding of Christ's body, so that they can grow and flourish in accord with the spirit of their founders.

Any institute of perfection and its individual members can be removed from the jurisdiction of the local Ordinaries by the Supreme Pontiff and subjected to himself alone.[217] This is possible by virtue of his primacy over the entire Church. He does so in order to provide more adequately for the necessities of the entire flock of the Lord and in consideration of the common good.[218] In like manner, these communities can be left or committed to the charge of their proper patriarchical authorities. In fulfilling their duty toward the Church in accord with the special form of their life, the members of these communities should show toward bishops the reverence and obedience required by canonical laws. For bishops possess pastoral authority over individual churches, and apostolic labor demands unity and harmony.[219]

By her approval the Church not only raises the religious profession to the dignity of a canonical state. By the liturgical setting of that profession she also manifests that it is a state consecrated to God. The Church herself, by the authority given to her by God, accepts the vows of those professing them. By her public prayer she begs aid and grace

217. To correct the impression that papal exemption withdraws the members of an exempt order from obedience to the hierarchy, the Constitution stresses that they are directly subject to the Pope himself: in addition they are, in certain respects further specified in the Decree on the Bishops' Pastoral office in the Church, subject to the local Ordinary. Exemption is a privilege granted for the sake of more effective service in the interests of the universal Church.

218. Cf. Leo XIII, constitution "Romanos Pontifices," May 8, 1881: Acta Sanctae Sedis 13 (1880-1), p. 483; and Pius XII, allocution "Annus Sacer," Dec. 8, 1950. AAS 43 (1951), pp. 28 f.

219. Pius XII, allocution "Annus Sacer," as cited in the preceding footnote, p. 28: the same Pontiff's apostolic constitution "Sedes Sapientiae," May 31, 1956: AAS 48 (1956), p. 355; and the allocution of Paul VI, as cited in footnote 210, pp. 570-1.

from God for them. She commends them to God, imparts a spiritual blessing to them, and accompanies their self-offering with the Eucharistic sacrifice.

46. Religious should carefully consider that through them, to believers and non-believers alike, the Church truly wishes to give an increasingly clearer revelation of Christ.[220] Through them Christ should be shown contemplating on the mountain, announcing God's kingdom to the multitude, healing the sick and the maimed, turning sinners to wholesome fruit, blessing children, doing good to all, and always obeying the will of the Father who sent Him.[221]

Finally, everyone should realize that the profession of the evangelical counsels, though entailing the renunciation of certain values which undoubtedly merit high esteem, does not detract from a genuine development of the human person.[222] Rather by its very nature it is most beneficial to that development. For the counsels, voluntarily undertaken according to each one's personal vocation, contribute greatly to purification of heart and spiritual liberty. They continually kindle the fervor of charity. As the example of so many saintly founders shows, the counsels are especially able to pattern the Christian man after that manner for virginal and humble life which Christ the Lord elected for Himself, and which His Virgin Mother also chose.

Let no one think that by their consecration religious have become strangers to their fellow men or useless citizens of this earthly city. For even though in some instances religious do not directly mingle with their contemporaries, yet in a more profound sense these same religious are united with them in the heart of Christ and cooperate with them spiritually. In this way the work of building up the earthly city can always have its foundation in the Lord and can tend

220. The true meaning of the religious life cannot be grasped except in relation to Christ, whose ministries the religious seek to mirror and to perpetuate.
221. Cf. Pius XII, encyclical "Mystici Corporis," June 29, 1943: AAS 35 (1943), pp. 214 f.
222. The Council here replies to two charges commonly directed against the religious life—that it impedes the full development of personality and that it cuts one off from effectively helping his fellow man.

toward Him. Otherwise, those who build this city will perhaps have labored in vain.[223]

In summary, therefore, this sacred Synod encourages and
praises the men and women, brothers and sisters, who in
monasteries, or in schools and hospitals, or on the missions,
adorn the Bride of Christ. They do so by their unswerving
and humble loyalty to their chosen consecration, while ren-
dering to all men generous services of every variety.

47. Let all who have been called to the profession of the
vows take painstaking care to persevere and excel increasingly in the vocation to which God has summoned them. Let
their purpose be a more vigorous flowering of the Church's
holiness and the greater glory of the one and undivided
Trinity, which in Christ and through Christ is the fountain
and the wellspring of all holiness.

223. *Cf. Pius XII, allocution "Annus Sacer," as cited in footnote 218,
p. 30; and the same Pontiff's allocution "Sous la maternelle protection,"
Dec. 9, 1957: AAS 50 (1958), pp. 39 f.*

Notes

CHAPTER ONE—THE MOVEMENT IS FORWARD

1. "World History and Salvation History," *The Christian and the World*. P. J. Kenedy & Sons, 1965, p. 47.
2. New York *Times,* June 23, 1966.
3. See Lichten. *Sister Formation Bulletin.* Spring 1966, p. 19.
4. Mother Mary Ambrosia, SSND. June *Circular* 49/66.
5. Abbott, *The Documents of Vatican II,* xvii, Guild Press, New York, 1966.
6. *Ibid.,* p. 27.
7. *Ibid.,* p. 29.
8. *Ibid.,* p. 32.
9. Harvey Cox. *The Secular City.* Macmillan, 1965, p. 158.
10. "Confutation of Tyndale's Answer," as quoted in *The Heart of Thomas More.* Ed. by E. E. Reynolds, Templegate, 1966, pp. 124-25.

CHAPTER TWO—A SPLENDID HERITAGE

1. Hubert Van Zeller, OSB. *The Benedictine Nun.* Helicon Press, 1965.
2. For an appreciative study of the high seriousness and spiritual aspiration of non-Christian creeds see R. C. Zahner, *Christianity and Other Religions,* Hawthorn Books, 1964.
3. John Henry Newman. *Essays Critical and Historical, XI: Milman's View of Christianity,* Vol. II, p. 233.
4. Alban Butler. *Lives of the Saints.* Burns & Oates, London, 1956.
5. Amelia Gere Mason. *Women in the Golden Ages.* Century, 1901, p. 226.
6. *Catholic Herald Citizen,* September 17, 1966.
7. *Ecclesiastical History,* Book 4, Chapters 7-10.
8. Decree on Renovation of Religious Life, #6.
9. Eckenstein, pp. 136-37.
10. *Ibid.,* p. 239.

11. *Ibid.,* p. 8.
12. *Ibid.,* p. 198.
13. Rev. H. J. Schroeder, OP. *Cannons and Decrees of the Council of Trent.* Herder, 1941, pp. 220-21.
14. *Ibid.,* p. 221.
15. Huyghe, *op. cit.,* p. 7.
16. Pope Leo XIII. *Conditae a Christo,* December 8, 1900. Catholic Encylopedia, Appleton ed. 1911, Vol. 12, p. 752.
17. Those with a statistical bent may be interested in the following data compiled from the *Guide to the Catholic Sisterhoods in the United States,* Thomas P. McCarthy, csv, ed. Catholic University of America Press, Washington, 1963.

Africa	2 congregations established in U.S., 20th century.
America	1 congregation in 18th century, 57 in 19th century, 44 in 20th century.
Asia Minor	2 congregations established in U.S., 20th century.
Austria	5 congregations established in U.S., 20th century.
Belgium	5 congregations established in U.S., 2 in 19th century, 3 in 20th century.
Canada	19 congregations established in U.S., 9 in 19th century, 10 in 20th century.
Central America	1 congregation established in U.S., 20th century.
China	2 congregations established in U.S., 20th century.
Czechoslovakia	1 congregation established in U.S., 20th century.
England	8 congregations established in U.S., 4 in 19th century, 4 in 20th century.
France	72 congregations established in U.S., 2 in 18th century, 42 in 19th century, 28 in 20th century.
Germany	38 congregations established in U.S., 30 in 19th century, 8 in 20th century.
Holland	4 congregations established in U.S., 20th century.
Hungary	5 congregations established in U.S., 20th century.
India	1 congregation established in U.S., 20th century.
Ireland	9 congregations established in U.S., 4 in 19th century, 5 in 20th century.
Italy	37 congregations established in U.S., 1 in 18th century, 8 in 19th century, 28 in 20th century.
Lithuania	3 congregations established in U.S., 20th century.

Mexico	6 congregations esablished in U.S., 20th century.
Poland	6 congregations established in U.S., 1 in 19th century, 5 in 20th century.
Russia	2 congregations established in U.S., 20th century.
South America	3 congregations established in U.S., 1 in 19th century, 2 in 20th century.
Switzerland	6 congregations established in U.S., 3 in 19th century, 3 in 20th century.
Spain	11 congregations established in U.S., 1 in 18th century, 3 in 19th century, 7 in 20th century.
Sweden	1 congregation established in U.S., 20th century.

CHAPTER THREE—FOCUS OF CHANGE IN RELIGIOUS LIFE

1. Mortimer Adler. "God and Modern Man," *The Critic.* October-November, 1966, p. 19.
2. Sister M. Angelica Seng. "The Sister in the New City," *The Changing Sister.* Fides, 1965.
3. Milwaukee *Journal.* October 23, 1966.
4. Gustave Martelet, SJ. "The Church's Holiness and Religious Life," *Review for Religious,* 1966, p. 59.
5. *Ibid.,* p. 58.
6. *Ibid.,* p. 109.
7. De Lubac. *Catholicism.* Mentor, 1960, p. 192.

CHAPTER FOUR—THAT TROUBLESOME VOW OF OBEDIENCE

1. *Dignitatis Humanae* #8.
2. J. M. R. Tillard. "Religious Obedience, Mystery of Communion." *Review for Religious,* XXIV, January 1965, p. 71.
3. Sister Mary Hester, SSND. "That Troublesome Vow of Obedience." *The Critic,* October-November 1965, pp. 47-49.
4. Karl Rahner. "Reflections on Obedience." *Cross Currents* X, fall 1960, p. 373.

CHAPTER FIVE—"HAVING NOTHING WE POSSESS ALL THINGS"

1. *Perfectae Caritatis,* #13.
2. Abbott, p. 475.
3. *The Christian Today.* Desclee, 1960, p. 138.
4. Pie-Raymond Régamey, PP. *Poverty.* Sheed and Ward, 1950, p. 18.
5. Sister Bertrande Meyers. "Who Is Sick Among Us." *Thought,* autumn 1966, pp. 366-80.
6. Arthur McCormack. *World Poverty and the Christian.* Hawthorn, 1963, p. 19.
7. *Perfectae Caritatis,* #13.

8. B. M. Chevignard. *Gospel Spirituality*. Sheed and Ward, 1965, p. 157.
9. Thomas Merton. *Thoughts in Solitude*. Farrar, Straus and Cudahy, 1958, p. 61.
10. Daniel Berrigan. "Who is Deprived." *Commonweal*, April 2, 1965, p. 55.

CHAPTER SEVEN—CHASTITY IS LOVE

1. Charles A. Schleck, csc. "The Sister in the Church." *Review for Religious*, January 1961, XX, p. 17.
2. Andrew Greeley. *The Hesitant Pilgrim*. Sheed and Ward, 1966.
3. *Ibid.*, p. 243.
4. Teilhard de Chardin. *The Making of a Mind*. Harper and Row, 1961, p. 149.
5. *Ibid.*, p. 233.
6. Dom Hubert Van Zeller. *More Ideas for Prayer*. Templegate, 1967, p. 11.
7. *Commonweal*, LXXXV, January 27, 1967, p. 450.
8. Pius XII. "Duties of Woman in the Social and Political Order." October 21, 1945.
9. Sister Elaine Marie Prevallet. "The Meaning of Virginity." *America*, July 23, 1966, pp. 93-95.
10. *Ibid.*, p. 94.
11. *Nun's Newsletter*, nccij, September 1966.
12. *Perfectae Caritatis*, #12.

CHAPTER EIGHT—THE SISTER IN FORMATION

1. Joseph H. Fichter. *Religion as an Occupation*. University of Notre Dame, 1961, p. 90.
2. Pius XII. "International Congress of Teaching Nuns." *Tablet* CIIC, September 22, 1951, p. 196.
3. Pius XII. "Address of Pope Pius XII to Religious Superiors." *Review for Religious* XI, November 1952, p. 306.
4. Sister Rose Dominic Gabisch, scl. *History of the Sister Formation Conference*. Unpublished manuscript, Sister Formation Conference, August 1966.
5. Donald McDonald. "Teaching the Teachers." *Commonweal*, LXIV, July 6, 1956, pp. 345-47.
6. Sister Mary Emil. *The Mind of the Church in the Formation of Sisters*. Fordham University Press, 1956.
7. Fichter, *op. cit.*, p. 112.
8. Mother Thomas Aquinas Carroll, rsm. "Everett Revisited, 1956-1966." *Sister Formation Bulletin*, autumn 1966, p. 14.
9. Sister M. Brideen Long, osf. "An Evaluation of Catholic Elementary School Teachers Pre-Service Education—A Follow-Up." *Sister Formation Bulletin*, autumn 1966, pp. 1-9.
10. *Ibid.*, p. 8.
11. Sister Mary Emil, ihm. "What Is Sister Formation?" *America*, X, January 12, 1957, p. 412-14.

12. Sister Rose Dominic. "Blueprint for the Future." *Sister Formation Bulletin,* XII, autumn 1965, p. 1.

CHAPTER NINE—AFTER VATICAN II

1. New York *Times,* April 28, 1967, p. 37.
2. "Norms for the Implementation of the Decree of the Second Vatican Council 'Perfectae Caritatis'" I, 3. *Sister Formation Bulletin,* autumn 1966, pp. 25-29.
3. *Perfectae Caritatis, #2.*
4. *America,* April 1, 1967, p. 490.
5. *Catholic Herald Citizen,* May 6, 1967, p. 11.
6. *The School Sister,* winter 1967, pp. 2-29.
7. Sister Rosemary Hudon, sos. *Nuns, Community Prayer and Change.* Alba House, 1967.
8. *Ibid.,* Preface.
9. Leon Joseph Cardinal Suenens. *The Nun in the World.* Tr. by Geoffrey Stevens. Palm Publishers, 1963, p. 122.
10. *SFC Bulletin,* autumn 1966, p. 27.
11. *Pastoral Constitution on the Church in the Modern World,* #59.
12. *Gaudium et Spes, #60.*
13. *Inter-Provincial News Letter,* March 1967, p. 4.
14. *Ibid.,* p. 4.
15. *Catholic Herald Citizen,* May 6, 1967, p. 5.
16. *A Nun's Newsletter,* March 1967.
17. *Perfectae Caritatis, #17.*
18. *America,* April 1, 1967, p. 492.
19. *Inter-Provincial News Letter,* December 1966, p. 2.

Index

Adelheid, Sister, 116
Adeltrudis, St., 30
Adler, Mortimer, 40
Adolfs, Father Robert, 38
Aethelburg, 29
Ahern, Father, 119
Amand, St., 29–30
Ambrosia, Mother, 13
America, 115
American Catholic Sociological
    Society, 28
Anderson, Rev. O. V., 117
Angelica Seng, Sister M., 42
Anita, Sister Mary, 93
Anna, 27
Annunciation Greek Orthodox
    Church, 116
Appropriate Renewal of the
    Religious Life, Decree on, 7
Aquila, 27
Araujo Sales, Bishop Eugenio de,
    115
Arrupe, Father Pedro, 124
Augustine, St., 32

Bastos, Mother Irany, 115
Beaconsfield, Council of, 29
Becket, Thomas à, 90
Bede, the Venerable, 29
Bells of St. Mary's, The, 44
Benedict, St., 28, 32, 119
Benedict XIV, Pope, 34
Berrigan, Father Daniel, 66–67
Berthold, Brother, 31–32
Bertrande Meyers, Sister, 60
Bettina, Sister Mary, 94–95
Boniface, St., 29
Boniface VIII, Pope, 32
Boylan, Father, 90
Brazil, nuns in, 115–116
Brideen Long, Sister M., 103–104,
    106
Bridget, St., 28

Caedmon, 29
Cardinale, Archbishop Igino, 31
Carrabine, Father Martin, 65
Carroll, Mother Thomas Aquinas,
    103, 107
Catholic hospitals, 20, 25
Catholic schools, 20, 25
    Ursuline, 34
Catholic Worker movement, 61
Change in religious life, 39–46
Chastity, vow of, 76, 77, 86–95
Chaucer, Geoffrey, 33
Chevignard, B. M., 63
Chevrier, Pére, 59–60
Christ, Jesus, 27, 45–46
Christ Church (Mequon, Wisc.),
    117
Clare, St., 32, 58
Cloistered contemplative life, 68–85
Clothing, *see* Religious garb
Cogley, John, 62
Columban Sisters, 109
Commonweal, 91
Concordia Lutheran Seminary, 117
Conditae a Christo, 34
Conferences of Major Superiors of
    Women, 18, 54

Constitution on the Sacred Liturgy,
    118
Contemplative life, cloistered,
    68–85
Convents
    beginning of, 27–29
    cloistered, 32–33
    missionaries and, 29–30
    schools in, 30
Corita, Sister, 43
Council, Vatican, *see* Second
    Vatican Council
Council of Beaconsfield, 29
Council of Trent, 33
Council of Whitby, 29
Cousins, Archbishop William E.,
    117
Cox, Harvey, 23–24
Cradle Song, 92
Critic, The, 49
Criticism of change, 17–18
Curie, Madame, 13
Cuthbert, Sister M., 72

Danielou, Father Jean, 59
Danielson, Pastor, 117
Daughters of Charity, 33, 42
Day, Dorothy, 61
Declaration on Religious Freedom,
    47
*Decree on the Apostolate of the
    Laity*, 65
*Decree on the Appropriate Renewal
    of the Religious Life*, 7, 17, 19,
    21, 27–28, 39, 74, 127–145
De Pauw, Father, 18
Discalced Carmelites, 73
Document on Adaptation, 8
Dogmatic Constitution on the
    Church, 21, 39, 90, 146–152
Dominic, St., 32
Dorcas, 27
Dupuy, Pierre, 109

Ealdham, 30
Ecclesia, De, 19, 21, 22
Education
    nuns and, 35, 44
    See also Catholic schools
Eglantyne, Dame (fictional char-
    acter), 33
Elaine Marie Prevallet, Sister, 92
Eliot, T. S., 90
Emerson, Ralph Waldo, 97
Emil, Sister Mary, 101–102, 105
English Virgins, 34
Eucharist
    mystery of, 21
    offering of, 22
Everett curriculum, 104–107
Expansion of commitments, 24–25

Faisal, King of Saudi Arabia, 19
Fasting, 72
Fichter, Joseph H., 98
First International Congress of
    Teaching Sisters in Rome, 100
For Heaven's Sake, Mr. Allison, 44
Ford Foundation Fund for the
    Advancement of Education, 105
Formation of nuns, 96–108

Foucauld, Charles de, 58
Francis, St., 32, 58
Francis de Sales, St., 33, 120
Franciscan Sisters, 107
Gambari, Father Elio, 55, 106
Gandhi, Mohandas K., 57
Gertrude of Helfta, St., 30
Gilbert, Rabbi Arthur, 116
Goldbrunner, Father, 119
Grace Miriam, Sister, 106
Greeley, Father Andrew, 28, 89
Guam, nuns in, 19

Habits, see Religious garb
Häring, Father Bernard, 61, 65, 118, 119
Harper, Father Jean, 95
Harper's Magazine, 49
"Harvest of Shame" (film), 64
Hawthorne, Mother Rose, 36
Herr, Dan, 87
Herrad, 31
Hilda of Whitby, St., 29
Hildegard of Bingen, St., 30
Histoire d'une Âme, 49
History of religious, 26–38
Hroswitha, 30
Hudson Institute, 38
Huyghe, Bishop Gerard, 33

Idung, 32
Ignatius, St., 91
Immaculate, Sister Mary, 43
Immaculate Heart College, 43, 63
Immigration of religious, 34–35
In the Likeness of Christ (Leen), 18
Institute of the Blessed Virgin Mary, 42
Inter-provincial Educational Conference, 13
Irany Bastos, Mother, 115
Ireland, 28

Jacob di Rivoli, St., 31
Jane Francis de Chantal, St., 33
Jerome, St., 28
Jerome Marie, Sister, 125–126
John, Bishop of Hexham (later of York), 29
John, St., 27
John XXIII, Pope, 16, 71
John the Baptist, 75
John of Beverley, St., 29
John of the Cross, St., 77, 96
John F. Kennedy Center for the Performing Arts, 43
José, Sister, 93
Jung, Carl, 38

Kaam, Father Van, 119
Kahn, Dr. Herman, 38
Kennedy, John F., 79

Lachman, Pastor Max, 116
Langland, William, 60
Latourette, Dr. Kenneth S., 117
Le Fort, Gertrude von, 79
League of Women Voters, 37
Leen, Father, 18
Lenten black fast, 72
Leo XIII, Pope, 34
Levites in Old Testament, 21–22
Lewis, C. S., 59
Life Magazine, 49

Lioba, St., 29, 30
Lipshitz, Rabbi, 117
Little Sisters of the Poor, 62, 94
Liturgy, Sacred, 21
Long, Sister M. Brideen, 103–104, 106
Look Magazine, 49
Lord, Rev. Daniel A., 14
Loyola University, 115
Lubac, Father Henri de, 46
Luce, Clare Boothe, 13
Luke, St., 27
Lumen Gentium, 110, 112
Lydia, 27

Madeleva, Sister, 58
Madonna, Sister Mary, 93
Mary Magdalen, 27
Major Superiors, National Conferences of, 8
Marillac, Louise de, 33
Marquette University, 116
Martelet, Father, 46
Martin of Tours, St., 28
Marygrove College, 101
Marymount College, 93
Masters, Edgar Lee, 96
Matthew, St., 59, 69
Mays, Pastor, 116
Medicare, 20
Medieval nuns, 28–33
Mequon, Wisc., 117
Mercedes, Sister Maria, 64
Merton, Thomas, 64, 119
Meyers, Sister Bertrande, 60
Mind of the Church in the Formation of Sisters, The (Sister Mary Emil), 102
Missionaries, 29–30
Missionary Church, 22–23
Missionary Servants of the Most Blessed Trinity, 107
Modern Woman, 13
More, St. Thomas, 25
Mortification, 71–73, 119–120
Mount Carmel Lutheran Church, 116
Murray, Father John Courtney, 119
Mystici Corporis, 73

National Association for the Advancement of Colored People, 37
National Catholic Council for Interracial Justice, 37
National Catholic Conference for Interracial Justice Traveling Workshop, 93, 123
National Catholic Directory, 87
National Catholic Education Association, 37
National Catholic Reporter, The, 15, 31, 110
National Conferences of Major Superiors, 8
National Union of Italian Superiors, 20
New Orleans, La., 16, 34
New Testament, 21
New York Times, 42
Notre Dame of the Lake, 117
Notre Dame of Maryland, 100
Novices, 58
Nun in the Modern World, The (Suenens), 40, 54

Nuns, Community Prayer and
    Change, 118
Nun's Story, The, 44
Nursing
    nuns and, 36
    See also Catholic hospitals

Obedience, vow of, 47-56
Old Testament, 21
Operation Upward Bound, 36
Ottumwa Heights College, 102

Padon Baptist Church, 117
Pastor, Rabbi Henry B., 116
Paul, St., 27, 88
Paul VI, Pope, 73, 125
    on religious life, 20–21
Paula, St., 28
Pauw, Father De, 18
Penance, 71–73, 120
Perfectae Caritatis, 94, 110, 112,
    115, 121
Periculoso, 32
Peter, St., 27
Peter Fourier, St., 33
Phoebe, 27
Pius XII, Pope, 45, 68, 70, 73, 92,
    100–101
Poor, Identification with, 62–63
Poor Clares, order of, 32
Post-Reformation Church, 33–34
Poverty, vow of, 57-67, 75, 121–122
Prayer, 77–78, 118–119
Prevallet, Sister Elaine Marie, 92
Printing press, 31
Prisca, 27
Professional training, 98–108

Rahner, Father Karl, 17, 56, 119
Réalités Magazine, 49
Régamey, Father, 59
Religious, defined, 26
Religious freedom, 47–48
Religious garb, 32, 124–126
Remy, Sister Mary, 43
Ritamary, Sister, 102
Ryan, Mary Perkins, 20

Sacred Congregation of Religious,
    8, 15, 19
Sacred Liturgy, 21
Salaries, 103
Sales, Bishop Eugenio de Araujo,
    115
Sales, St. Francis de, 120
San Francisco, Calif., 16
Schillebeeckx, Father E., 119
Schleck, Father, 89
Scholastica, St., 28
School Sisters of Notre Dame, 12–13,
    33, 41, 52, 63, 87, 107, 113, 117,
    123
    Rules and Constitutions of the
        Congregation of, 22
School Sisters of St. Francis, 42,
    123
Screwtape Letters (Lewis), 59
Second Vatican Council, 22
    nuns and, 14
    adaptation of, 109–125
    religious congregations and, 39,
        41
Secular City, The (Cox), 23
Sedes Sapientia, 106
Self-identity, 20

Seng, Sister M. Angelica, 42
Shalom, Temple, 116
Simeon, 27
Singing Nun, The, 44
Sister Formation Bulletin, The, 105,
    108
Sister Formation Movement, 19, 44,
    101–108, 114
Sisters of the Assumption of the
    Blessed Virgin Mary, 35
Sisters of Charity of St. Vincent de
    Paul, 107
Sisters of the Holy Cross, 107
Sisters of Jesus Crucified, 36
Sisters of Notre Dame, 107
Sisters Spiritual Institute (1966),
    116
Sleep, 73
Slum conditions, 23
Social service, nuns and, 36–37
Spiritual reading, 119–120
Sponsa Christi, 68
Stergiardes, John, 116
Suenens, Leo Joseph Cardinal, 40,
    54, 118
Syllabus of Spirituality (Gambari),
    106

Teilhard de Chardin, Father Pierre,
    14, 91
Teresa, Sister, 76, 96
    on contemplative life, 68–85
Teresa of Avila, St., 32, 70
Thecla, 27
Theresa, Mother, 12–13
Thérèse of Lisieux, St., 49, 76
Thomas, Dylan, 46
Thomas, St., 72
Thomas Aquinas Carroll, Mother,
    103, 107
Thomas More Association, 87
Time Magazine, 49
Traditions in community, 14–16,
    18
Trent, Council of, 33

Ursuline order, 33
    in New Orleans, 34

Vatican Council, see Second Vatican
    Council
Vestal Virgins, 26
Vietnam War, 26
Vincent de Paul, St., 33, 45
Virginity, 94–95
Vocations of nuns, 122–124
    education, 35–36, 44
    nursing, 36
    social service, 36-37
Vow of chastity, 76, 77
Vow of obedience, 47–56
Vow of poverty, 57–67, 75, 121–122

Walburgis, St., 30
Wanderer, The, 110
Ward, Mary, 33
Weigel, Father Gustave, 119
Werburg, Queen, 29
Whitby, Council of, 29
White Sister, The, 49
Whitman, Walt, 97
Wihtred, King, 29
Winebald, St., 30

Zeller, Father Van, 26, 91